THE SCIENCE AND
TECHNOLOGY OF
Ben
Franklin

Poor Richard, 1737.
AN
Almanack
For the Year of Chrift
1 7 3 7,
Being the third after LEAPYEAR.

ALICIA Z. KLEPEIS

ILLUSTRATED BY
MICAH RAUCH

Titles in the **Build It Yourself Science Biographies** Set

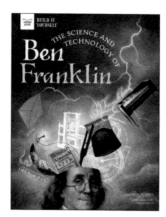

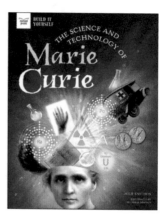

Check out more titles at www.nomadpress.net

Nomad Press

A division of Nomad Communications

10 9 8 7 6 5 4 3 2 1

This book was manufactured by CGB Printers,
North Mankato, Minnesota, United States
May 2021, Job #1018285
ISBN Softcover: 978-1-64741-018-6
ISBN Hardcover: 978-1-64741-015-5

Educational Consultant, Marla Conn

Questions regarding the ordering of this book should be addressed to
Nomad Press
PO Box 1036, Norwich, VT 05055
www.nomadpress.net

Printed in the United States.

CONTENTS

**Interested in
Primary Sources?
Look for this icon.**

Use a smartphone or tablet app to scan the QR code and explore more! Photos are also primary sources because a photograph takes a picture at the moment something happens. You can find a list of URLs on the Resources page. If the QR code doesn't work, try searching the internet with the Keyword Prompts to find other helpful sources.

🔎 Benjamin Franklin

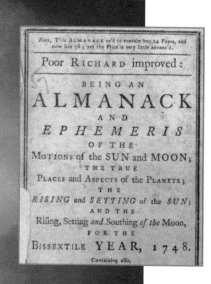

1706: Benjamin Franklin is born on January 17 in Boston, Massachusetts.

1717: Eleven-year-old Franklin invents swim fins.

1718: Franklin begins an apprenticeship in his brother James's printing shop.

1728: Along with partner Hugh Meredith, Franklin opens his own printing shop in Philadelphia, Pennsylvania.

1731: Franklin founds the Library Company of Philadelphia, the country's first subscription library.

1732: Franklin publishes his first *Poor Richard's Almanack*.

1736: Franklin's 4-year-old son, Francis, dies of smallpox.

c. 1739–42: Franklin invents the Pennsylvania fireplace.

1748: Franklin retires from the printing business.

1750: Franklin invents the lightning rod.

1751: Franklin's book *Experiments and Observations on Electricity*, is published in London, England.

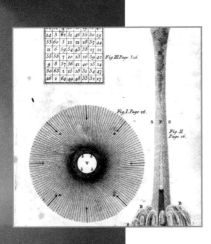

1752: Franklin conducts his famous kite experiment, proving that lightning is electricity.

1757: Franklin goes to England to serve as a London representative of the Pennsylvania Assembly.

1761: Franklin invents the glass armonica.

1775: The Second Continental Congress appoints Franklin the first U.S. postmaster general.

1776: Franklin travels to France in the role of American commissioner to France.

1784: Franklin invents bifocals.

1786: Franklin's map of the Gulf Stream is published in the *Transactions of the American Philosophical Society.*

1786: Franklin invents the long arm to reach books on high shelves.

1787: Franklin serves as delegate to the Constitutional Convention and signs the U.S. Constitution.

1790: Franklin dies on April 17 in Philadelphia at the age of 84.

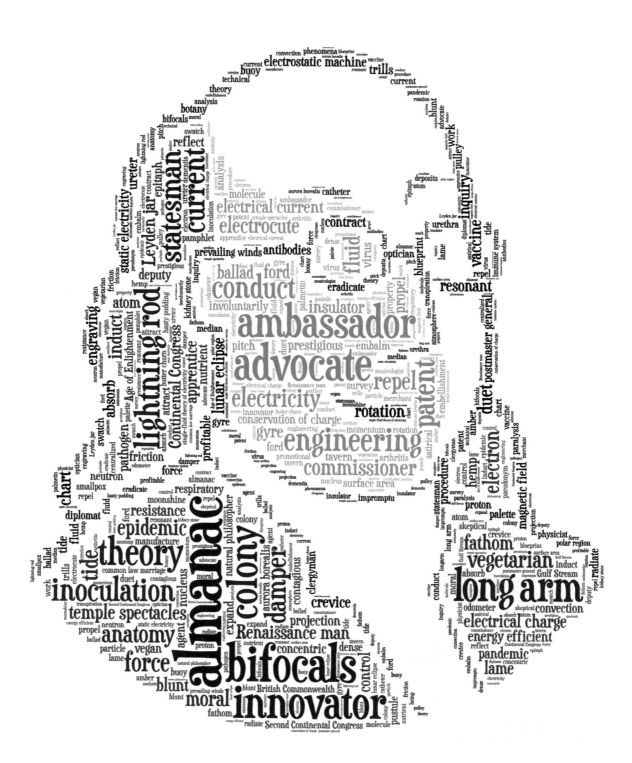

MEET BENJAMIN
FRANKLIN

HELLO! MY NAME IS BENJAMIN FRANKLIN. MAY I ASK WHAT YEAR IT IS?

2021. DO YOU MEAN YOU ARE "THE" BENJAMIN FRANKLIN?

YES, IT IS "I"! I HAVE TRAVELED INTO THE FUTURE TO SEE WHAT WONDERS HAVE SPRUNG UP IN THIS GREAT COUNTRY OF MINE!

Ding!

Candlemaker. Printer. Firefighter. Diplomat. Inventor. Scientist. At some point in his life, Benjamin Franklin (1706–1790) did all of these very different jobs. In fact, it wasn't unusual for him to juggle several different careers at a time. How did he manage such a feat?

Ben Franklin had many things going for him. For one thing, he was a hard worker. He was also endlessly curious. Ben's enthusiasm for learning was a constant from the time he was just a boy . . . and it really never diminished.

In some ways, Ben Franklin was born in the perfect time period to be curious. The **Age of Enlightenment**, also called the Age of Reason, took place from about 1680 to 1820. This was a period when people asked all kinds of questions about nature, government, society, religion, and, of course, what we now call science.

ESSENTIAL QUESTION

What is Benjamin Franklin famous for?

1

WORDS TO KNOW

diplomat: a person who represents one country to another.

Age of Enlightenment: the time period when European scientists and philosophers started to examine the world using reason rather than religion.

theory: a set of ideas to explain something that has happened.

natural philosopher: the term once used to describe people interested in science.

statesman: an experienced political leader.

clergyman: a male religious leader, such as a minister or priest, particularly a Christian one.

pseudonym: a pen name, or fictitious name used by an author.

Back in Franklin's time, the word "scientist" didn't even exist. Those who did experiments and tested **theories** were known as **natural philosophers**. No matter what the label, Benjamin Franklin was a man of amazing accomplishments. Want to know more? Let's rewind a few centuries . . . .

THE LIFE OF BEN

Benjamin Franklin was born in Boston, Massachusetts, on January 17, 1706. He was one of 17 children! In 1712, the Franklin family moved to a bigger home. In this building, Franklin's father, Josiah, also had his candle- and soap-making shop. Young Ben Franklin read from an early age. He read everything, from the Bible to what he could find in his dad's small home library.

Famous Farts

Known as one of America's Founding Fathers, Benjamin Franklin is famous for his work as a **statesman**. He helped write both the Declaration of Independence and the U.S. Constitution. But did you know that he also wrote an essay about farting and sent it to the Royal Academy of Brussels? It's true! The academy was looking for people to submit scientific papers, and Mr. Franklin answered its call. He suggested that scientists should research how to make a medicine that would make farts smell "agreable as perfumes." Even though this essay may seem silly, it fits in with Benjamin Franklin's overall goal of solving practical, everyday problems through science. It also shows that this brilliant man had a sense of humor.

When Ben was a child, young boys in Boston had lots of free time. They didn't go to school and they didn't have to work at real jobs. In fact, Ben had only two years of formal education in his entire life! At age 8, he went to a school called Boston Latin, where he studied Greek and Latin among other subjects. But after just one year, his dad decided not to enroll Franklin for the next school year. It's likely that Josiah Franklin decided Ben was not really cut out to be a **clergyman**—the aim of his education.

Ben Franklin, 1785

Credit: Joseph Duplessis (1725–1802)

"Benjamin Franklin is the **FOUNDING FATHER** who winks at us."

—Walter Isaacson, biographer

Silence Dogood

In 1721, Benjamin's brother James Franklin (1697–1735) started his own newspaper called *The New-England Courant*. Teenager Ben Franklin disguised his handwriting and slipped an essay he'd written under the door of James's printing house. Ben chose the **pseudonym** Silence Dogood for the piece. Mrs. Dogood was supposed to be a widow of middle age—nothing like the sassy, teenaged boy Ben really was. Silence Dogood's writings were witty and covered a range of topics. They also boosted sales. Late in 1722, Ben told his brother who the real Silence Dogood was. Not surprisingly, James was not pleased.

 You can read an article by Silence Dogood at this website. Does it sound like something a teen would write?

🔍 Mass hist Silence Dogood

WORDS TO KNOW

apprentice: a person who works with a master to learn a skill or trade.

lunar eclipse: when the moon, earth, and sun are all lined up in a row so that the earth casts a shadow on the moon.

colony: an area that is controlled by or belongs to another country.

moral: concerned with principles of wrong or right behavior.

electricity: energy created by the movement of electrons between atoms. An atom is a tiny particle of matter. Electrons are particles in an atom that have a negative charge and move around.

After Boston Latin, Ben spent one year at a math and writing school that his father thought would help him in future business matters. And that was the end of Ben's schooling. Do you think Benjamin Franklin would have liked to continue his education? What subjects do you think he would like to study if he were at your school?

Silence Dogood **WASN'T THE ONLY PEN NAME** Ben Franklin used during his life. He also tried Richard Saunders, Anthony Afterwit, Polly Baker, Alice Addertongue, Caelia Shortface, Martha Careful, Busy Body, and Benevolous.

At age 10, Ben found himself working full-time in his dad's candle and soap shop. He hated it. It was hot, smelly work. When he was 12, Ben became an **apprentice** to his older brother James, who was a printer. Ben worked hard setting type one letter at a time and carrying trays of heavy, cast-metal letters.

A 1914 reproduction of a Charles Mills painting by the Detroit Publishing Co. of Benjamin Franklin at work on a printing press

Benjamin Franklin headed to New York, New York, in September 1723. Unfortunately, when he arrived, he could not find work as a printer. He moved again, to Philadelphia, Pennsylvania. A year later, Pennsylvania Gov. William Keith (1669–1749) sent him to London, England, to get printing equipment to bring back to Philadelphia to set up his own shop. But it turned out that the governor didn't actually have the money to pay for the equipment. Did Franklin give up? No! He made the best of a tough situation. He worked for printers in London. But he also saw plays and met up with friends for meals and fun.

In London, Franklin read all kinds of books and had great conversations with others in coffeehouses. Benjamin Franklin hoped to meet the great scientist Isaac Newton (1643–1727), though sadly, that never happened.

"During Franklin's life, the average person never traveled more than 20 MILES from their home. Franklin . . . spent 27 YEARS of his life overseas."
—Jamie Spatola, writer

Community Driven

In 1727, Franklin founded a club called the Junto. The word *junto* means "together" in Spanish. What was the purpose of this club? Its members sought to improve both themselves and their community. The initial 12 members came from different lines of work, from a self-taught mathematician to a shoemaker. They met each week to discuss current events, books they'd read, **moral** issues, and more. Can you think of ways people do this today?

On the trip home in 1726, Franklin's curiosity and passion for science kept him busy. He did experiments on crabs he'd found living on seaweed. He used the timing of events during a **lunar eclipse** to figure out how far he was from London. He also observed and studied the behaviors of marine creatures he saw on the voyage, including flying fish and dolphins.

Back in the **colonies**, Benjamin Franklin established his own print shop and bought a newspaper, the *Pennsylvania Gazette*. This paper became the most successful one in all the American colonies! It had news, of course, but also letters from readers, gossip, and humor. Later in life, Franklin used his paper to share scientific information, such as the results of his experiments with **electricity**.

WORDS TO KNOW

common law marriage: a marriage through living together for the long term rather than by a civil or religious ceremony.

almanac: a reference book containing information such as weather forecasts, lists and tables, moon phases and tide charts, short articles, and household tips.

tide: the daily rise and fall of the ocean's water level near a shore.

survey: to examine and record the features of an area of land in order to construct a map or a plan.

botany: the study of plants.

phenomena: events, facts, or features of scientific interest that can be observed.

agent: a person who does business or acts on behalf of others.

commissioner: an official in charge of a government department.

Continental Congress: the group of delegates from the American colonies who met during and after the American Revolution. They issued the Declaration of Independence and Articles of Confederation.

In 1730, he entered into a **common law marriage** with Deborah Read (1708–1774). Two years later, 1732, was a huge year for Benjamin Franklin. In October, Deborah gave birth to a son and at the end of the year, Franklin published the first version of his *Poor Richard's Almanack*. What's an **almanac**? It's a reference book with information on topics from the **tides** to weather forecasts. But Ben Franklin's almanac was also full of humor. Poor Richard Saunders, whom the almanac was named after, was a fictional character. Every year, people would buy a new almanac—after all, the times of the tides and weather forecasts changed from year to year. Franklin published *Poor Richard's Almanack* for 25 years. It made him a fortune.

About **10,000 COPIES** of *Poor Richard's Almanack* **were sold each year!**

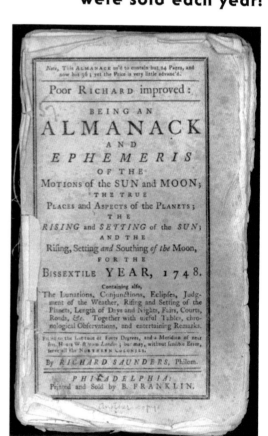

Poor Richard's Almanack

SCIENTIST AND INVENTOR

In 1743, Benjamin Franklin started the American Philosophical Society (APS). Its members included scientists and other big thinkers from Philadelphia and beyond.

What was the society's purpose? "Promoting useful knowledge." This knowledge included a little of everything. Finding better ways of curing or preventing diseases. Creating new maps and **surveys** of land. Improving what people knew about math and **botany**. The APS also encouraged experimentation to help people understand the world, including natural **phenomena**, around them.

Political Life

During the course of his life, Benjamin Franklin played a huge role in shaping the future of the nation. He worked to unite the colonies and served twice as an **agent** for several colonies in London. There, he voiced the concerns of the American colonists when speaking to members of England's Parliament. When the American Revolution (1765–1783) broke out, he was sent to serve as **commissioner** to France. He was also a member of the **Continental Congress**, signer of the Declaration of Independence, and framer of the Pennsylvania Constitution and the U.S. Constitution.

embalm: to preserve a body.

physicist: a scientist who studies physical forces, including matter, energy, and motion, and how these forces interact with each other.

In 1748, Franklin chose to retire from his printing business so he'd have more time to devote to his scientific studies. That was a bold move for a 42-year-old man whose business was a raging success.

Benjamin Franklin's home became a laboratory and invention space. Franklin often merged science and invention. For example, when he was researching electricity, he sometimes made instruments from materials he had around the house. Franklin was not looking for fame or fortune when creating his new devices or home improvements. He simply wanted to make peoples' lives easier and better. Sometimes, Benjamin Franklin invented devices all on his own. Other times, he improved on the inventions of other people.

Could Science Bring Ben Franklin Back to Life?

Benjamin Franklin dreamed of being able to see America 100 years into the future. He once wrote that he wished there was a way to **embalm** people so they could come back to life later. He went on to say that rather than an ordinary death, he'd like to be "immersed in a cask of Madeira wine, with a few friends till that time, to be then recalled to life by the solar warmth of my dear country!" But he recognized that such a dream was probably unrealistic since he lived in a time "too near the infancy of science."

As with his printing business, Ben Franklin's scientific pursuits were incredibly successful. In 1753, London's Royal Society awarded him the gold Copley Medal. This would be like winning a Nobel Prize for science today!

Franklin was also awarded honorary degrees from a number of institutions, including Harvard, Oxford, Cambridge, and Yale. So, despite only having two years of formal schooling, Benjamin Franklin became Dr. Franklin.

UNTIL THE END

Franklin defied the odds of aging, continuing to research and travel into his 80s. In October 1776, the elderly Franklin boarded a speedy ship to France. Even though he was in France to negotiate a peace treaty to help end the American Revolution, he also made time to meet with scholars. He chatted with the chemist Antoine Lavoisier (1743–1794), the **physicist** Alessandro Volta (1745–1822), and members of France's Royal Academy. Wanting to encourage scientific conversations, Franklin established a group called the Société Apollonienne, similar to the American Philosophical Society back in Philadelphia.

Franklin made his final voyage across the Atlantic in 1785. During the trip, he jotted down 40 pages of notes on many topics related to the ocean: how to improve the design of boats, how to conduct experiments that gauge the wind—using playing cards. He also wrote down ideas about building better stoves and fixing smoky chimneys.

FRANKLIN'S RECEPTION AT THE COURT OF FRANCE, 1778.
RESPECTFULLY DEDICATED TO THE PEOPLE OF THE UNITED STATES

Benjamin Franklin continued to read about science and ask questions until his death on April 17, 1790. Franklin's funeral was a huge event with about 20,000 people in attendance.

Franklin's reception at the court of France, 1778
Credit: Anton Hohenstein, 1823-1909

WORDS TO KNOW

procedure: a series of actions performed in a specific order.

Franklin greatly expanded peoples' understanding of electricity, of course, but also of the importance of science to solve everyday problems. He showed a concrete example of the value of giving back to one's community. His constant desire to learn and willingness to educate himself were inspiring. Many of his inventions and scientific discoveries are still part of daily life for people around the globe. Let's take a closer look at how Franklin's work affects us today!

Good Science Practices

Every good scientist keeps a science journal!

Scientists use the scientific method to keep their experiments organized. Choose a notebook to use as your science journal. As you read through this book and do the activities, keep track of your observations and record each step in a scientific method worksheet, like the one shown here.

Question: What are we trying to find out? What problem are we trying to solve?

Research: What is already known about the problem?

Hypothesis/Prediction: What do we think the answer will be?

Equipment: What supplies are we using?

Method: What **procedure** are we following?

Results: What happened? Why?

Each chapter of this book begins with an essential question to help guide your exploration of Benjamin Franklin and his work. Keep the question in your mind as you read the chapter. At the end of each chapter, use your science journal to record your thoughts and answers.

ESSENTIAL QUESTION

What is Benjamin Franklin famous for?

EXPERIMENT WITH
HOMEMADE SOAP

Back when Ben Franklin was a kid, making soap was a smelly affair. It's much easier—and more fun—today. Have an adult help you with the knife and the hot glycerin (soap).

Caution: An adult must help you melt the glycerin.

❯ **Spray the inside of your ice cube trays or plastic cups with cooking spray.**

❯ **Cut a small chunk (about the size of a couple of ice cubes) of glycerin from the block.** Place the glycerin into the measuring cup or bowl. Heat on high in the microwave for 30 seconds. If any of the glycerin is still solid, continue heating just until the glycerin is melted. It should not be boiling.

❯ **Ask an adult to take the melted glycerin out of the microwave.** If using the dye, add a drop or two to the melted glycerin. Use the craft stick to stir so the dye is mixed in. Repeat with a drop or two of the essential oil, if using.

❯ **Have an adult pour the liquid glycerin into the molds or plastic cups.** Leave the soap in the molds until it completely hardens. Pop it out and enjoy!

CACHE KIT

° silicone ice cube trays or plastic cups
° vegetable cooking spray
° microwave-safe measuring cup or a Pyrex bowl
° block or bar of solid glycerin (available at craft stores)
° knife
° craft stick
° colored soap dyes, essential oils (optional)

Think Like Ben!

Test your soap against other kinds of soap. Try dish soap, laundry soap, and shampoo. Are they similar? How are they different? Which kind gets your hands cleaner? Which gets cloth and other materials cleaner? Use your science journal to keep track of your observations.

TEXT TO **WORLD**

Does your family or classroom use an almanac to help track the weather and other natural events? If so, how well does it predict things? If not, what do you use instead?

Chapter 1

THE SCIENCE OF
SPARE TIME

AS I RECALL, YOU ENJOY A VERY ACTIVE LIFE, DON'T YOU, MR. FRANKLIN?

THAT IS TRUE! ESPECIALLY SWIMMING. I DEVELOPED MANY OF MY OWN TECHNIQUES AND DEVICES TO HELP ME SWIM FASTER.

YOU SHOULD COME SCUBA DIVING WITH ME TODAY!

Playing sports and having fun are things kids do today. You might play baseball and softball on a field on a spring day. You might catch a basketball game at the gym on a winter afternoon. But, when Ben Franklin was a boy, these sports hadn't even been invented yet! So, what did he do for fun? Water sports!

ESSENTIAL QUESTION

If an invention doesn't work as planned, is it a failure or a success? Why?

Water sports were some of Ben's favorite activities. He grew up near the Charles River in Boston and really enjoyed swimming and boating. When out on a boat or canoe with his friends, he was often the person in charge because his skills were good.

DIVE IN

Today, many kids take swim lessons. But swimming wasn't a popular activity in Colonial America. Franklin lived long before people had heated swimming pools or shark watchers for ocean beaches. So, Ben Franklin had to teach himself. He was always willing to try new things and develop new skills. In true Franklin fashion, he taught his friends how to swim, too.

Ben Franklin did not wear ANY CLOTHES when swimming!

Many kids would have been satisfied to just swim with their friends. But not Ben Franklin. He wondered how he might swim faster. First, he thought like a scientist. He noticed a connection between how big a person's hands and feet were and how much water they could push to **propel** themselves while swimming. Bigger hands move more water.

How do this person's fins move them through the water?

WORDS TO KNOW

palette: a thin, normally oval board with a thumb hole at one end, used by artists to lay and mix paints.

surface area: the total area that the surface of an object occupies.

force: a push or a pull that causes a change of motion in an object.

momentum: a force that keeps an object moving after it has begun to move.

resistance: a force that opposes or slows down another force.

Next, young Ben thought like an inventor. He made swim paddles out of wood. Each was shaped like a painter's **palette** with a hole for the thumb. The paddles were about 10 inches long and 6 inches wide. Did these paddles work? Yes and no. Franklin later wrote that the paddles helped him swim faster, but made his wrists tired.

Franklin also built flippers for his feet. He described them as "a kind of sandals" that fit onto his soles. But after trying them out, he discovered that it wasn't just the soles of his feet that were responsible for the swimming strokes. His ankles and the insides of his feet were also essential to propulsion.

Swim paddles were Benjamin Franklin's first invention. He was only 11 years old at the time. Even though they were not 100-percent successful, his process was spot on. He thought about a question and built an invention to achieve his goal. Then, he tested his invention and discovered ways to improve it. This is what scientists and inventors do today.

The Science & Design of Swim Paddles

Benjamin Franklin wrote in his autobiography about how hand paddles helped him to swim faster. But how do they work? Swim paddles add **surface area** to a swimmer's hands. This allows swimmers to use more **force**—to "grab" more water, which creates more forward **momentum** when they pull their hands through the water. Today, people use swim paddles to strengthen their muscles. The paddles add increased **resistance** to their muscles as they catch and pull the water. But paddles have changed a lot since young Ben Franklin made his own. For example, swim coach Jim Montrella designed a plastic version of swim paddles in the 1970s. They were rectangular in shape and had special tubing that held the middle finger and wrist to the paddle. Even though many other varieties of swim paddles have been created since then, Montrella's design is still available today.

EXPERIMENTS & EXHIBITIONS

So what if young Franklin's swim paddles weren't a definitive success? That didn't stop him from continuing to experiment with water and motion. He sent a kite up into the air and then waded into a pond while holding the string. With the string still in hand, he began to float on his back. Can you guess what happened? The kite started to pull him across the pond. He was delighted with this easy mode of travel.

Clever Franklin even figured out that he could affect his speed by adjusting the length of the kite string. He later recalled, "I was only obliged occasionally to halt a little in my course, and resist its progress, when it appeared that by following too quick, I lowered the kite too much; by doing which I occasionally made it rise again."

The Thames River does not have super-clean water. Many people who swam long distances in the Thames got sick afterward. In 2011, comedian David Walliams (1971–) got an intestinal infection called giardia after swimming there.

Body Positive

When people today think of Benjamin Franklin, they often picture him as a somewhat plump, older man. But as a young man, he was quite fit—and not especially shy about showing off his body. He swam in London's Thames River on many occasions, showing off his spectacular swimming skills and strokes. Biographer Walter Isaacson writes, "At 17, Franklin was physically striking: muscular, barrel-chested, open-faced, and almost 6 feet tall."

Ben Franklin's love of the water continued when he moved to England as a young man. He had questions about different swimming motions and strokes. He did some reading on the topic to learn more. One book he studied was *The Art of Swimming*. Franklin was interested in perfecting his swim techniques both on the surface and underwater. He also taught friends to swim, just as he had back in Boston.

The River Thames around 1750
Credit: Canaletto (1697–1768)

Franklin had a friend named Oliver Neave who was afraid to learn to swim as an adult. Franklin suggested an experiment. He told Neave to try wading into a body of water until the water was about chest height. He told his friend to toss an egg back toward shore, where the water was a little shallower. Franklin said Neave should dive for the egg while keeping his eyes open. Why? To discover that the water **buoys** a person up and that it's harder to sink than he might have imagined.

What SPORTS or other forms of EXERCISE have you tried? Do any of them make you more tired than others?

In 1726, Franklin was boating with friends on the Thames when he decided to jump into the river and go for an **impromptu** swim. He swam all the way from Blackfriars to Chelsea, about 3.5 miles. Along the way, he did tricks above and below the water's surface. People watching were delighted with his feats. Franklin was offered the chance to run his own swimming school. But this was one of the few jobs he chose not to try!

Swimming World magazine has a video of a Benjamin Franklin impersonator talking about how he learned to swim, when he swam in the Thames, and how he nearly became a swim instructor. **Check it out!**

🔎 Swimming World Ben Franklin

PS

OTHER ATHLETIC PURSUITS & BELIEFS

Swimming wasn't the only sport Benjamin Franklin participated in. Later in life, he developed a routine of lifting weights. This was quite unusual during a time when many people worked physically all day on farms. They weren't heading to the gym to work out!

Dr. Charlene Gamaldo, the medical director of the Johns Hopkins Center for Sleep, said, "We have solid evidence that exercise does HELP YOU FALL ASLEEP more quickly and IMPROVES SLEEP QUALITY."

Ben Franklin exercised into old age, partly because he thought scientifically about the connections between exercise and health. He believed that by working out, people could help prevent disease.

Based on his own experience, Franklin wrote that an evening swim caused him to sleep well all night long. Hundreds of years later, scientists now support Franklin's personal findings. What sports or other forms of exercise have you tried? What makes you feel healthiest?

Swimming and weightlifting were not the only forms of recreation Franklin enjoyed. Another was music.

Founding Father, Famous Swimmer

In 1968, Benjamin Franklin was **inducted** into the International Swimming Hall of Fame. Not only was he a good swimmer and skilled teacher, but he also gave good advice about water safety, the use of lifeboats to rescue people from shipwrecks, and the importance of learn-to-swim classes. He thought of swimming more as a valuable life skill than a sport. He proposed that all schools in the **British Commonwealth** have swimming programs.

WORDS TO KNOW

trills: rapid alternations between one tone and another, often performed on a long note of a song.

skeptical: doubting the truth or value of an idea or belief.

ballad: poetic verses set to song.

resonant: continuing to produce sound.

MUSICAL MERRIMENT

Benjamin Franklin often found ways to connect his interests and hobbies with science and invention. Music was a great example of this. Did Franklin have a musical mind? Absolutely!

Franklin liked Scottish folk songs and simpler tunes. He didn't really go for the popular music or the modern operas of his time. While he didn't quite use science to explain his musical preferences, he did have logical explanations of what he liked—or didn't like—about various musical selections. For instance, he would criticize how some composers of his day set words to music. He didn't like when people broke up words with **trills** or other vocal showboating.

Balloon Mania

Franklin was interested in many different things beyond swimming, exercise, and music, such as balloon travel! The first hot air balloon flight took place in France in June 1783. While Ben Franklin didn't see this initial flight, he saw a balloon ascent later that year. This flight left from Paris—with passengers onboard—and traveled about 5.5 miles. Franklin wrote in his journal, "We observed it lift off in the most majestic manner. When it reached around 250 feet in altitude, the intrepid voyagers lowered their hats to salute the spectators. We could not help feeling a certain mixture of awe and admiration." Even though some folks were **skeptical** about the point of hot air balloons and their usefulness, Franklin thought experimenting for curiosity's sake came first and practical uses for these objects would eventually follow. So, when a fellow spectator asked him about the use of a hot air balloon, he replied, "What is the use of a newborn baby?"

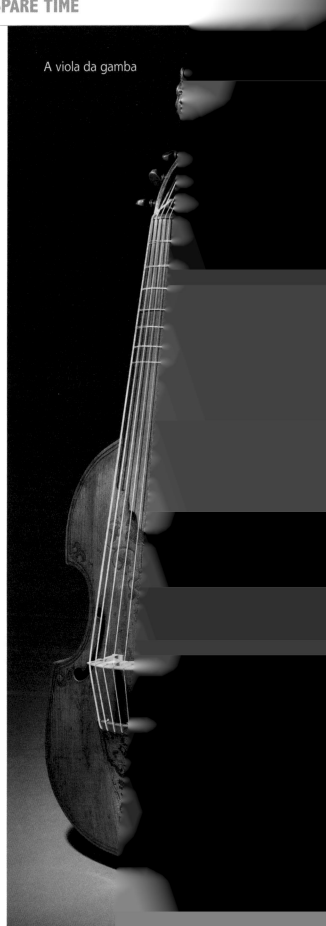

A viola da gamba

Do you play any instruments? Ben Franklin did. He played the harp and the guitar. He also played the viola da gamba, a stringed instrument similar to a cello.

Benjamin Franklin was even a musical creator. He wrote songs about people he knew and the times he was living in. He wrote one **ballad** about a famous pirate named Blackbeard. Another tune, called "My Plain Country Joan," was about his wife, Deborah.

A MUSICAL INVENTION

Between 1757 and 1775, Benjamin Franklin spent much of his time working in England. While there, he attended many social gatherings. Dinner guests who were bored often made music using just wet fingers and the rims of their glasses. Running a wet finger along the rim of a glass makes a **resonant** sound.

Have you ever made a glass sing? **Find out how it works in this video!**

🔎 Mocomi singing glass

PS

WORDS TO KNOW

pitch: the lowness or highness of a sound.

While in England, Franklin even went to a concert where the music was performed on wineglasses. He was captivated by how beautiful these glasses sounded.

Many people go to concerts, listen to the tunes, and that's the end of the story. But not Ben Franklin. The inventor in him was intrigued after the wineglass performance.

A colleague in the Royal Society had also done a demonstration for Franklin using glasses and water. The glasses were fixed to a table and filled with varying amounts of water. When he slid wet fingers around the rims, the glasses made different sounds depending on how full they were. Franklin found this interesting but thought it was awkward to try to play upright glasses. The wheels in his brain started turning.

Could he create his own glass music maker that was more convenient to play? Yes! In 1761, he invented a new musical instrument—the glass armonica.

The name "armonica" comes from the Italian word *armonia,* meaning "harmony." Franklin believed his new instrument would be **WELL-SUITED** to play Italian music.

WHAT IS A GLASS ARMONICA?

Benjamin Franklin had many skills. But he wasn't a glassblower. He worked with a London glassblower named Charles James. James made a few dozen glass bowls for the armonica. Unlike water glasses, where the level of water determines the notes you can play, the bowls in Franklin's armonica didn't need water. They were made of varying sizes and thicknesses so each one had a unique **pitch**. Franklin even color-coded the bowls with paint so that each one represented a different note. Clever!

The armonica had 37 bowls. Each one had a hole in its center. An iron rod went through all the holes in the bowls to keep them in place. But how did Franklin keep the bowls from cracking into each other? He put corks between them.

A glass armonica. Which bowls produce a higher sound?

The rod was attached to a wheel, which was connected to a foot pedal. When Franklin pressed on the pedal, the wheel turned and the bowls spun. Then, he made music by touching the spinning bowls with damp fingers.

Watch composer William Zeitler (1954–) demonstrate how a glass armonica is played. Can you think of any similar instruments?

🔎 Smithsonian Franklin Invention

PS

WORDS TO KNOW

absorb: to soak up something, such as a liquid, or take in energy, heat, light, or sound.

engineering: using science, math, and creativity to design and build things.

THE GLASS ARMONICA: GOOD, BAD & CREEPY

Ben Franklin had a terrific time with his invention. The glass armonica was fragile, but he still took it with him when traveling and enjoyed playing it for others.

The glass armonica grew in popularity. Soon, it wasn't just Franklin who was playing this instrument. Several people playing the armonica were women, which was unusual for the time. Even Queen Marie Antoinette (1755–1793) of France took lessons! Famous composers including Beethoven (1770–1827) and Mozart (1756–1791) wrote pieces of music for Franklin's invention. Amazing!

> "Of all my inventions, the **GLASS ARMONICA** has given me the greatest personal satisfaction."
> —Benjamin Franklin

Are Armonicas Evil?

Even though Benjamin Franklin was delighted with his armonica, not everyone liked it. In the decades after its invention, some upsetting events were linked to this instrument. Some musicians who played the armonica complained of feeling dizzy or nervous. Others experienced cramps and muscle spasms. Some listeners experienced problems after simply hearing Franklin's invention. After a child died during an armonica performance, the instrument was even banned in some German towns. What could have caused these negative effects on people? Some folks thought the armonica's high-pitched notes summoned spirits of dead people. Others thought these tones could cause madness in listeners or even had magical powers. A perhaps more scientific, yet also unproven, hypothesis was that lead found in the glass or paint of the armonica's bowls could have been **absorbed** into the fingers of musicians playing the instrument, making them sick.

So, what does the glass armonica sound like? Benjamin Franklin's wife once referred to it as "the music of the angels." Some described its sound as haunting. Others said it was like a watery organ. And similar to a piano, the musician can play multiple notes at the same time.

MORE THAN 5,000
glass armonicas had **been built by the time** Ben Franklin died.

Although the glass armonica became popular pretty quickly, it was practically forgotten by the 1820s. The reasons aren't entirely clear, but perhaps it was because the instrument was hard to transport or because its sound was a bit creepy. We may never know the real reason, but if you watch the Harry Potter movies, you'll get to hear one!

As fun as it was to apply science and **engineering** to sports and music, Franklin was also obsessed with other areas of study—heat and light. We'll learn more in the next chapter!

ESSENTIAL QUESTION

If an invention doesn't work as planned, is it a failure or a success? Why?

TEXT TO **WORLD**

How can you apply science and engineering to the sports you play or the hobbies you have?

GO FURTHER AND FASTER:
DESIGN SWIM PADDLES

Ben Franklin invented swim paddles. But several other inventors created new and different versions of them. What would your ideal set of swim paddles look like?

❯ **Before designing, go online or read books to see what kinds of paddles exist.** Maybe you'd like to create a totally new type of paddle. Engineers often come up with several designs before deciding which is best. Sketch all your design ideas!

❯ **Gather materials.** Collect things that are easy to find—perhaps even recycled items you have at home. What features of your paddles will help keep them secured while swimming?

❯ **Build and test your paddles.** Go to a local swimming pool with an adult. Time yourself swimming the same distance with and without the paddles. Do they work well? If not, how could you alter them to improve their performance? Would a different material change how your swim paddles work?

Think Like Ben!

To go with your swim paddles, could you design swim fins for your feet?

Follow the Engineering Design Process

The engineering design process is a great way of keeping track of your progress whenever you invent something. Follow the steps and record your designs and observations in your science journal so you can look back to check your progress.

› **Problem:** What problem are you trying to solve?

› **Research:** Has anything been invented to help solve the problem? What can you learn?

› **Question:** Are there any special requirements for the device? An example of this is a car that must go a certain distance in a certain amount of time.

› **Brainstorm:** What new designs or materials could you try? Go wild!

› **Prototype:** Pick a promising idea and build a model.

› **Test:** Test your prototype and record your observations.

› **Iterate:** Use test results to improve your idea. Repeat the steps to create the best solution possible!

DESIGN A
NEW INSTRUMENT

Ben Franklin came up with many new ideas during his lifetime. In this activity, you'll design and create your own musical instrument. You can use any materials. What will your instrument sound like?

❱ **Take some time to think about the type of instrument you'd like to make.** It could be a wind or percussion instrument, one with strings, or perhaps something no one has ever seen. Sketch out your ideas in your science journal.

❱ **Dig around at home to come up with some supplies to build your instrument.** Can't find exactly what you had in mind? That's okay—some of the best inventions come from thinking outside the box.

❱ **Start building your instrument.** Does it look how you'd imagined? What sound does it make? If you are not happy with its early appearance or sound, how can you improve it?

Franklin's String Quartet?

Many people believed that Franklin composed a string quartet sometime around 1778. It's an unusual piece of music that uses a technique where the instruments (violins and cello) are retuned to produce a different sound than normal. A French **musicologist** found the manuscript in the 1940s. So, what's the issue? The manuscript shows Franklin's name listed as the author, but the handwriting is not his. Also, the name *Franklin* is spelled incorrectly. Was the piece any good? That depends on the reviewer. One person called the composition "a miserable work." Ouch!

 Want to hear it and make your own judgment? **Check out this link.**

🔎 Franklin Institute musical talent

Think Like Ben!

After you build your instrument, can you find a way to change its pitch? Can you design another instrument to accompany the first one so you can play a **duet** with a friend?

WORDS TO KNOW

musicologist: a person who studies music.

duet: a musical composition written for two performers to play.

25

Chapter 2

HEAT &
LIGHT

HAVE THERE BEEN ANY IMPROVEMENTS TO MY FIREPLACE AND STREETLAMP DESIGNS?

MOST HOMES DON'T RELY ON FIREPLACES ANYMORE AND STREETLAMPS USE ELECTRICTY. ELECTRICITY IS A BIG PART OF HEATING HOMES AND CARS.

AMAZING! SO, IS THIS A CAR? I AM VERY INTRIGUED. CAN WE GO FOR A RIDE?

Clothing colors. Candle flames. Fireplaces. Streetlights. At different times in his life, Benjamin Franklin was curious about all of these things. How are they connected? Think heat and light!

During the 1730s, Franklin conducted some of his earliest experiments on heat. In one experiment, he wanted to look at the effects of heat on different-colored fabrics. This turned out to be a classic example of how Franklin often started a scientific **inquiry**. He was curious about something and then later tried to come up with a practical use for what he discovered.

ESSENTIAL QUESTION

How are heat and light related to each other?

On a sunny morning, Franklin and another Junto member placed several small pieces of cloth on top of snow. They used several different colors: black, deep blue, lighter blue, purple, green, red, yellow, and white. Franklin allowed the cloth pieces to sit in the sun for a few hours. He wanted to discover which pieces absorbed the most heat from the sun's rays and which absorbed the least.

BLACK CLOTH ABSORBS
all of the colors of sunlight and reflects almost none.

WHITE CLOTH REFLECTS
the colors of sunlight and absorbs very little of it.

Franklin found that the black and dark blue **swatches** had sunk the most into the snow. The white fabric was still on the snow's surface. The two men measured how much snow had melted under each patch of fabric to determine how much the sun had heated each piece. What did they discover? The dark-colored fabrics absorbed more heat than the lighter ones.

Many years later, Ben Franklin wrote about these results in a letter to a friend. He came up with several practical ideas inspired by the colored fabrics experiment. One was that black clothes weren't as suitable to wear in a hot, sunny climate as white clothes were. Another was to paint the walls of fruit sheds black. Why? "To preserve the fruit from frosts" and to speed up their ripening process.

Not every idea Franklin had about fabric colors was 100 percent accurate. For example, he thought that people wearing black clothes in a hot climate would suffer from dangerous fevers. But that's part of science—not every idea is correct!

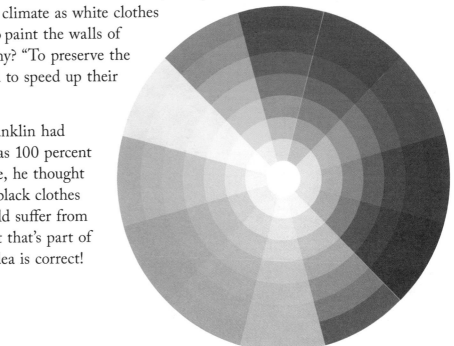

GLASS & HEAT

After finding out what happened to colored fabric placed on snow, Franklin repeated the experiment with a pane of glass. He was interested in learning more about the connections between glass, heat, and sunlight. How are these three things connected?

The glass pane sank into the snow. That might seem weird. After all, light is able to go right through a pane of glass. Later, people discovered that glass stops heat in its tracks even as it lets the light through. So, Franklin's glass pane warmed up and melted the snow underneath.

Franklin tried another experiment involving glass, heat, and sunlight. (You shouldn't try this at home because it is rather dangerous.) Franklin had a piece of glass that was hot from the sun. He focused the glass on two different pieces of paper. One was black, the other was white. Both the black and white pieces of paper eventually caught fire. Which paper do you imagine caught fire first?

A practical application for Franklin's discovery: a greenhouse!

The white paper took longer to catch fire than the black one. Just as with white fabric, the white paper absorbed less heat than the darker piece of paper, so it took longer to catch fire.

HEAT & FIRE

In twenty-first-century America, homes can be toasty warm and cozy in the wintertime. You can turn on the thermostat and instantly have heat. But, back in Ben Franklin's time, Colonial American homes were often dark, smoky, and cold. Sound cozy? A funny rhyme from the 1700s shares this experience:

A smoky fireplace and a nagging wife
Are two of the greatest ills in life.

Most houses in Ben Franklin's time had open fireplaces. Wood fires blazed inside these fireplaces. They also provided a spark to his scientific mind.

Have you ever sat in front of a fireplace? Does all the heat come straight out? Why or why not?

WORDS TO KNOW

expand: to spread out and take up more space.

property: a characteristic quality or distinctive feature of something.

contract: to shrink and take up less space.

Franklin wanted to improve the quality of indoor heating. But, before he could do that, he needed to find the answers to many questions. How does air flow? Can air flow be controlled? How does heat move? Franklin conducted his heat experiments in his home. He assumed that this space was full of air that would rise and **expand** when it was warm.

One experiment involved a candle and a keyhole. Franklin held a lit candle up to the keyhole of a door to his room. He wanted to see if the candle's flame bent toward the keyhole. If it did, he would know that heat was escaping through the hole. Today, scientists know that heat always moves from areas with higher temperatures to those with lower temperatures. Why did Franklin care about heat escaping through the keyhole? In the winter, no one wants a room or their home to lose heat.

Another heat experiment was to test the different **properties** of cold and warm air. Franklin heated an empty bottle, then put it upside down into water. As the air temperature inside the bottle decreased, the air inside **contracted**, or decreased in size. This created enough space for water to rise up inside the bottle. The experiment showed clearly that warm air takes up more space than cold air.

Using his newfound knowledge, Franklin went on to design one of his most famous inventions.

Firefighter Ben

During Colonial times, lots of homes and businesses were built from wood and heated with open fireplaces. People also used candles for light. As a result of so many open flames, fires ruined many a building in Colonial America. In 1733, Franklin wrote an article in the *Pennsylvania Gazette* in which he discussed the importance of having a group of citizens who would work to prevent and protect peoples' properties from fires. In 1736, Franklin founded the first volunteer fire company in America—the Union Fire Co. Initially, the company had about 25 members. They met monthly to talk about firefighting techniques. The group was a huge success. You could say that the idea of volunteer fire companies spread like wildfire!

FRANKLIN'S PENNSYLVANIA FIREPLACE

Through his experiments at home, Benjamin Franklin learned much about how heat moved. He knew that in the typical open fireplace of his day, lots of heat was lost when the warm air rose and went right up the chimney. This certainly didn't help someone sitting on the other side of the room.

Rooms containing open fireplaces were often drafty, too. As the warm air went up and out through the chimney, cold air rushed in to replace it. Another problem with an open fireplace was that smoke tended to drift out into the room. Not pleasant!

Franklin's drawing for what became known as the Franklin stove, 1744

Credit: Beinecke Rare Book & Manuscript Library, Yale University

Using his newfound knowledge, Franklin invented a new type of wood-burning stove, known as the Pennsylvania fireplace. His goal was to both maximize the heat in a room and minimize the smoke and drafts.

Home Science

Even though Franklin was an avid scientist, he didn't have his own separate laboratory. Instead, he used his entire home as a lab. For his experiments with air, he worked in an enclosed room. Working at home was inexpensive. It was also smart—anyone who read the results of his experiments could probably verify Franklin's findings if they wanted to, assuming they had rooms with fireplaces at home. Where have you done science experiments outside of a laboratory?

WORDS TO KNOW

energy-efficient: using less energy to provide the same results.

manufacture: to make into a product.

prototype: a working model or mock-up that allows engineers to test their solution.

conduct: to transfer something such as electricity or heat.

radiate: to spread outward.

pamphlet: an informative brochure or book.

promotional: relating to the publicizing of a product or venture to increase sales or boost public awareness.

engraving: a type of printing where the design is drawn or etched into the plate instead of the design being raised on the plate.

Franklin also hoped that his Pennsylvania fireplace would be more **energy-efficient**—that is, use less wood to heat a room than a traditional open fireplace. Why did this matter?

Just a few decades after the city of Philadelphia was founded, citizens had to get their wood for heat farther and farther outside the city as more trees were cut down and used for materials. No simple task when they had to transport the wood by horse and buggy. Is energy efficiency still a concern today? Why?

Benjamin Franklin employed the help of an ironworker named Robert Grace (1709–1766). Grace **manufactured** the first Pennsylvania fireplace, what we call a **prototype**.

How did the Pennsylvania fireplace work? It was a wood-burning stove designed to be built into a fireplace. At its most basic level, it was an iron box. The stove was built in such a way that heat and smoke from the fire rose up and warmed an iron plate located above it. The hot air was meant to travel through a series of metal chambers in back of the metal box.

History Mysteries

It may seem that historians know everything there is to know about Benjamin Franklin with complete accuracy. Historians, however, debate when the Pennsylvania fireplace was actually invented—and built. In his autobiography, Franklin says that he invented it in 1742. But some historians think it's more likely that he invented the Pennsylvania fireplace during the winter of 1739–40. In 1744, Franklin wrote that both his family and friends had enjoyed the warmth of his invention during the past four winters. Will we ever know for sure when the first Pennsylvania fireplace was used? Maybe not.

This helped prevent the heat from escaping. Since metal **conducts** heat well, the heat inside the metal box **radiated** into the room. The iron walls of this stove absorbed heat as the fire burned. It gave off warmth into the room for quite a while after the fire stopped burning. And it needed less wood to heat a room than an open fireplace.

PAMPHLETS, PATENTS & PROBLEMS

In the days before television and YouTube advertisements, how did inventors or businesspeople drum up business for their products? Many used **pamphlets** to show off their goods. In 1744, Ben Franklin came up with a **promotional** pamphlet for the Pennsylvania fireplace. His was a mixture of salesmanship and, of course, science. It included diagrams and **engravings** and was a slick publication for its time.

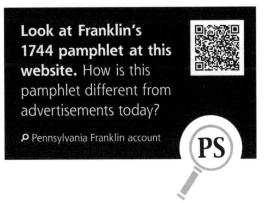

Look at Franklin's 1744 pamphlet at this website. How is this pamphlet different from advertisements today?

🔎 Pennsylvania Franklin account

WORDS TO KNOW

patent: a document given to the inventor of something that protects them from someone copying their invention.

convection: the transfer of heat from one region to another by the movement of a gas or liquid.

damper: a plate or valve that regulates the draft in a fireplace or stove.

Renaissance man: a person who has many areas of knowledge or talents.

Today, people often consider *An Account of the New Invented Pennsylvanian Fireplaces* as Benjamin Franklin's earliest scientific publication. It gave directions on how to assemble and use this new stove. It explained the science behind the movement of warm and cold air, as well as how smoke is carried by air and how heat radiates. In true scholarly form, the pamphlet connected its explanations to books on the subject of natural philosophy.

When it first went on sale, a Pennsylvania fireplace cost 5 pounds. In 2019, that would be about $1,081. Sales of the Pennsylvania fireplace were so good that Franklin became quite rich. The governor of Pennsylvania offered Franklin the chance to **patent** his invention. As with every invention he ever made, Franklin said no.

> "As we enjoy **GREAT ADVANTAGES** from the inventions of others, we should be glad of an **OPPORTUNITY** to serve others by any invention of ours; and this we should do freely and generously."
> —Benjamin Franklin

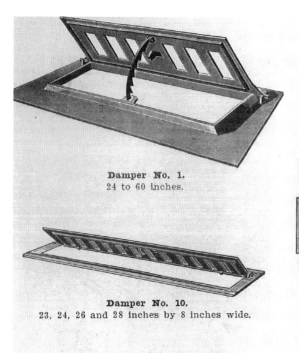

Damper No. 1.
24 to 60 inches.

Damper No. 10.
23, 24, 26 and 28 inches by 8 inches wide.

Was Franklin's Pennsylvania fireplace a total success? Absolutely not! Its design was flawed. The stove didn't have a source of fresh air to circulate through it. As a result, the fire tended to die out fast. And since there wasn't enough **convection** to keep the smoke from the fire rising up out of the chimney, it came out into the room.

> "The Pennsylvania fireplace was an **ONGOING EXPERIMENT**: Franklin would tinker with it for the rest of his life."
> —Joyce E. Chaplin, biographer

Despite the problems with his new invention, Franklin did not give up on it. During the late 1760s, for example, he created a movable metal plate called a **damper**. This could both channel the smoke into the chimney when the stove was on or close the fireplace off completely when it wasn't being used to avoid making the room drafty.

Other people tinkered with Franklin's design as well. One of the most important modifications to the stove was the work of David Rittenhouse (1732–1796), a friend and fellow inventor from Philadelphia.

David Rittenhouse

A true **Renaissance man**, David Rittenhouse was one of America's great inventors and scientists. Much like his friend Benjamin Franklin, Rittenhouse was largely self-taught. He was especially gifted in math and science. He set up a clock-making shop, though he was also known for making mathematical and surveying instruments. Some sources say Rittenhouse built the first telescope in the United States. As an astronomer, he is especially well-known for his detailed observations of the transit of Venus in 1769.

Much like Benjamin Franklin, Rittenhouse did a lot to help his country. He worked as the city surveyor of Philadelphia in 1774. He also surveyed the state boundaries between Pennsylvania and New York, New Jersey, Maryland, and Delaware. Rittenhouse served as the first director of the U.S. Mint. And after Franklin's death, he became the president of the American Philosophical Society.

WORDS TO KNOW

BCE: put after a date, BCE stands for Before Common Era and counts years down to zero. CE stands for Common Era and counts years up from zero. This book was published in 2021 CE.

innovator: a person who introduces new products, ideas, or methods.

crevice: a narrow opening, especially in a rock or wall or where two sides meet.

aurora borealis: a natural display of shimmering colors in the night sky, usually only seen in the far north. Also called the northern lights.

Rittenhouse added an L-shaped exhaust pipe, or chimney, to the Pennsylvania fireplace. The pipe allowed the smoke to rise up out of a home through the chimney. This new-and-improved model, eventually known as the Franklin stove, was much more efficient than Franklin's original stove.

LIGHTS, SCIENCE, ACTION!

If you walk at night in Philadelphia today, you don't usually need a flashlight. Streetlights illuminate the city. But in Ben Franklin's day, Philadelphia had no streetlights.

Franklin didn't invent the streetlight. Nor was he the first to use one in Philadelphia. So, what was the connection between Franklin and street lighting?

Franklin was an **innovator** who improved on the design of existing streetlamps. At the time, globe-style lamps were imported from London for use as streetlights. These lamps had wicks and were fueled by fish oil. But they weren't designed very well. No air came into the globe from below and smoke didn't easily come out from the top of the globe. As a result, smoke gradually filled up the globe, blocking the light from view.

Back in 500 BCE, the Chinese lit up the city of Beijing using VOLCANIC GAS FLOWING through bamboo pipes. Ancient Romans lit up their streets with oil lamps. And long before European cities had streetlamps, other cities, including Bagdad in Iraq and Córdoba in Argentina did.

Franklin's streetlamp had four flat panes of glass. This was a better design. If anything or anyone bumped into the globe-style lamp, the whole thing would break, but not so with the new four-pane design. Franklin's streetlamp also had a long funnel that drew the smoke upward and out of the lamp. **Crevices** let in air from below. Franklin had figured out that more airflow was needed within the glass globe to avoid the buildup of soot from the oil burning inside. This cleaner glass gave off more light than the London-style ones.

Philadelphia has 100,000 STREETLIGHTS today.

LIGHTS IN THE SKY

Benjamin Franklin's interest in light went beyond streetlights. He was also fascinated by the northern lights, or the **aurora borealis**. Many say this interest began during his journeys across the North Atlantic on his way to England. He first wrote about the colorful phenomenon in the *Pennsylvania Gazette* in 1737.

Have you ever seen the northern lights? **Take a look!**

🔎 northern lights YouTube

PS

What did Franklin think was behind these dazzling night lights?

THIS IS ASTOUNDING! AND ARE THOSE TODAY'S STREETLAMPS?

YEP, THEY ARE!

I BET THEY SHINE LIKE STARS IN THE NIGHT SKY!

THEY DO! SADLY, THAT'S LED TO SOMETHING CALLED "LIGHT POLLUTION," WHICH MAKES IT HARD TO SEE REAL STARS OVER HEAVILY POPULATED AREAS.

WORDS TO KNOW

electrical charge: a force of electricity that can be either positive or negative.

polar regions: the areas of the earth around the North and South Poles, within the Arctic and Antarctic Circles.

particle: a tiny piece of matter.

atmosphere: the blanket of air surrounding the earth.

atom: a very small piece of matter.

molecule: a group of atoms bound together to form matter.

magnetic field: an invisible area (or field) created by a magnet.

He thought the shifting lights were caused by **electrical charges** that were concentrated in the **polar regions** and were made more intense by snow and other moisture. He believed that this "overcharging" led to a release of electrical light into the air.

Was Ben Franklin correct in his explanation? Not really. It turns out that the northern lights appear in the sky when very small **particles** stream outward from the sun. When these particles hit Earth's **atmosphere**, they give some energy to the **atoms** and **molecules** found in the gases of the upper atmosphere. These atoms and molecules, however, can't hold on to all that energy, so they release it as a different kind of energy—light.

Franklin didn't stop at the northern lights when he thought about electricity. No, he was fascinated with how electricity worked back on Earth as well as in the sky. We'll take a look at his experiments with electricity in the next chapter.

ESSENTIAL QUESTION

How are heat and light related to each other?

Want to know more about the northern lights? **Check out the information at this website.**

🔎 Exploratorium auroras

Credit: U.S. Air Force photo by Staff Sgt. Joshua Strang

The colored lights known as the aurora most commonly occur around the NORTH AND SOUTH POLES. The particles entering Earth's atmosphere contain an electric charge. As they arrive, Earth's magnetic field directs them toward the poles.

COLOR & HEAT
ABSORPTION

Ben Franklin studied how different-colored fabrics were heated by the sun. Do all colors heat up at the same rate? In this experiment, you'll find out!

❯ **Fold each sheet of construction paper in half the long way.**

❯ **For each sheet of paper, tape one short end and the long end totally shut.** Your pieces of paper should look like pockets.

❯ **In your science journal, draw six lines from top to bottom so you have five columns.** Leave the first column without a heading. On the top of the other four columns, write the names of the colors you are using. Along the side of the paper, write "Measurement 1," "Measurement 2," "Measurement 3," and "Measurement 4." Leave some space between these labels so it's easier to write.

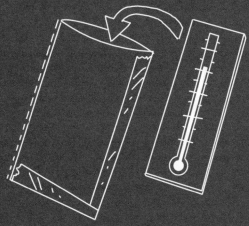

❯ **Take your pockets and thermometers outside to a sunny spot.** Record the starting temperature for each thermometer. Place one thermometer inside each of the construction paper pockets.

❯ **For one hour, record the temperature inside each of the pockets every 15 minutes.** Label the first temperature in the Measurement 1 row, and so on.

❯ **Look over your observations.** Did all of your thermometers heat up at the same rate? Did they end up having the same temperatures at the end of the hour?

Think Like Ben!

Try this experiment again. But instead of using pockets made of construction paper, place the thermometers inside different kinds of packing materials. How do your results differ? Which materials do you think would work best for shipping candy, for example?

TEXT TO **WORLD**
What applications can you think of for Franklin's fabric test?

LIGHT UP
THE NIGHT

Cities around the world have many different styles of streetlamps. The city of Minneapolis, Minnesota, alone has five styles of standard street lighting, with shapes such as an acorn, teardrop, and shoebox. What would your street lighting look like for a city of the future?

❯ **Research other streetlights from cities around the globe today.** Pay attention to their shapes, what they are made of, and which ones are the brightest or the coolest to look at.

❯ **In your science journal, sketch some designs for your streetlights.** Do you want to create an unusual design, one that blends into the city landscape, or one that gives off the most light? What shape do you think would work best in your neighborhood? Why? Do you think your street needs more light, more artistry, a design that discourages birds from landing on the lights, or something else? How does this inform your design?

❯ **Gather some materials from around your house that you could use to make a prototype of your streetlight.**

❯ **Build a prototype of your streetlight.** Test it with the mini LED candle so you can see how light shines out of it. Try it in your house to make sure it works and then bring it outside to test in different places.

❯ **What do you find needs changing in your design?** Did the streetlight cast enough light? Did it look appealing? How can you improve it?

Think Like Ben!

After you build a streetlight in one style, could you build a completely different one? Ask a group of friends or family members to vote on which one they'd prefer to see in a city of the future.

INSULATE IT!

Benjamin Franklin was interested in how heat moved and how to keep people warm. In this experiment, find out what materials are the best insulators—materials that don't easily allow heat to pass through or escape.

CACHE KIT

° assorted materials
° 4 glass jars with lids
° rubber bands or tape
° thermometer
° timer

❯ **Choose three different materials to use as insulation for your glass jars.** What materials do you think might keep the heat in best? This could be anything from bubble wrap to old fabric. Be sure you have enough of each material to wrap it around a jar three times. And be sure to get permission before you cut up any fabric!

❯ **Wrap each jar in one of the three materials you chose.** Use either rubber bands or tape to hold the material in place. The fourth jar will have no insulation around it. This is what scientists call a **control**. It's important to know what happens to the object that has nothing changed about it.

❯ **Fill each of your jars with the same amount of hot tap water.**

❯ **Using your thermometer, take the temperature of the water in each jar.** Each jar should start out the same. Record the results in your science journal.

❯ **Place all four jars inside the refrigerator.** Set your timer for 15 minutes.

❯ **Take the jars out after 15 minutes.** Use your thermometer to record the water temperature in each jar. Which one was the coldest? Which one stayed warmest? Which of the materials that you used might be best suited to use in a coat during the winter?

Think Like Ben!

Do the same experiment using different materials as insulation. What happens if you put the jars into the freezer instead of the refrigerator?

WORDS TO KNOW

insulator: a material that prevents heat, sound, or electricity from passing through it easily.

control: something used as a standard for comparison to check the results of an experiment.

Chapter 3

ZAP:
IT'S ELECTRIC!

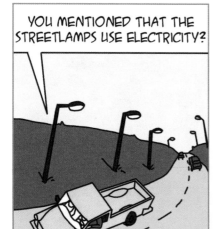

Think about your typical day. Does it start with an alarm clock going off? Perhaps you look at your cell phone that was charging overnight. From turning on the lights to making toast, electricity is part of many aspects of our everyday lives.

ESSENTIAL QUESTION

How did Ben Franklin change peoples' understanding of electricity?

When the power goes out, people experience what daily life was like back in Ben Franklin's time—at least in terms of electricity. But what exactly is electricity? And when did people, including Benjamin Franklin, start to understand this form of energy?

By the time Franklin began experimenting, not much progress had been made in understanding electricity since ancient times. More than 2,000 years before Ben Franklin, a Greek philosopher named Thales of Miletus (c. 624–546 BCE) wrote up his observations of what today we call **static electricity**.

Benjamin Franklin Drawing Electricity from the Sky, c. 1816
Credit: Benjamin West (1738–1820)

Thales conducted experiments by rubbing different materials against each other, such as cat fur and **hemp** against **amber**. He found that the **friction** from rubbing these materials against the amber caused the amber to attract lightweight materials, including ash and dust.

The word **"ELECTRICITY"** comes from the Latin word *electricus*, meaning "like amber."

WORDS TO KNOW

fluid: a substance such as a gas or a liquid that flows freely and has no fixed shape.

attract: a force that draws things closer.

repel: a force that pushes things away.

You may have experienced static electricity in ways you never knew. Have you ever walked across a carpeted floor and gotten a shock when you touched a doorknob or touched a blanket fresh out of the dryer and had it zap you a little? Those are both examples of static electricity.

So, how does static electricity relate to Ben Franklin? Let's go back to the year 1743 and find out.

FROM PARTY TRICKS TO PROPER SCIENCE

Today, scientists around the globe understand and study electricity, but back in Franklin's time, people often explained electricity by talking about **fluids**. Some scholars thought that electricity involved two different kinds of fluids, known as vitreous and resinous, which could be created separately. Vitreous fluid resulted from rubbing glass, and resinous fluid from rubbing resins such as amber. Scientists believed that objects that had different electrical fluids would **attract** each other, while objects with the same type of electrical fluid would **repel** each other. But this idea of electrical fluids wasn't right.

Watch professor Jim Al-Khalili recreate "The Hanging Boy Experiment." How might the reactions of audiences today be different from the audiences of Franklin's time?

🔎 BBC hanging boy jim

PS

Folks in Franklin's era certainly couldn't imagine a future where electricity would provide the world with power and light. Instead, electricity was seen as a mysterious force. Showmen even tinkered with it for entertainment. Such electrical entertainment sparked Franklin's imagination.

In 1743, Franklin went to a performance by Dr. Archibald Spencer (1698–1760), a scientist from Scotland. Among Spencer's tricks was one known as "The Dangling Boy," sometimes called "The Hanging Boy." In this stunt, a boy was suspended from the ceiling using silk ropes. While he hung there, another person would rub his feet with a big piece of smooth rounded glass, which drew sparks from the boy's hands or face.

What did this trick show? That the human body can conduct electricity.

Spencer's electrical performance captivated Franklin. He wanted to learn more about this mysterious force. A contact in London sent Franklin a long glass tube and papers that described how to perform some static electricity experiments.

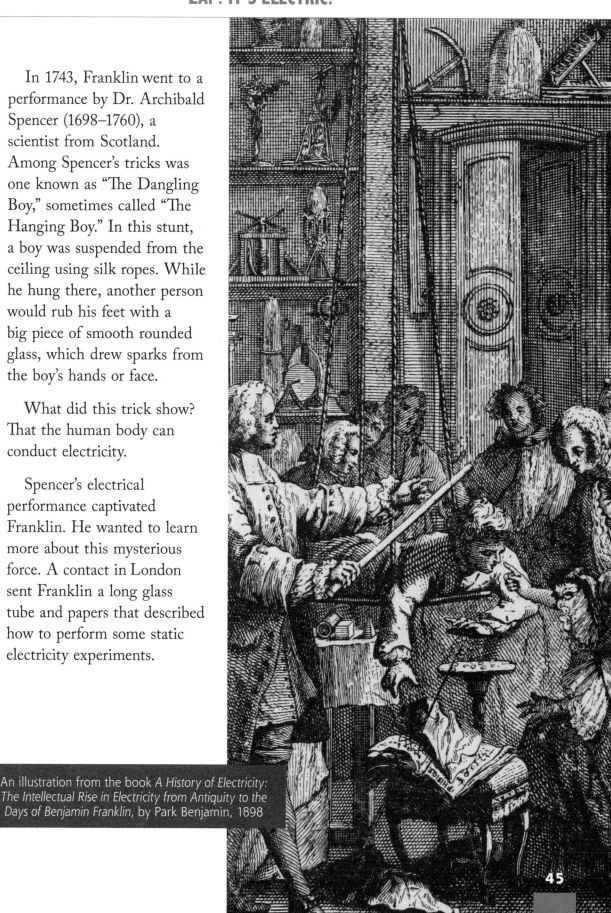

An illustration from the book *A History of Electricity: The Intellectual Rise in Electricity from Antiquity to the Days of Benjamin Franklin*, by Park Benjamin, 1898

WORDS TO KNOW

electrostatic machine: a machine used to generate sparks of electricity.

Leyden jar: a storage container for electricity made of glass, foil, and wire.

Franklin's electrostatic machine

Franklin wrote back, saying, "I never was before engaged in any study that so totally engrossed my attention."

Ben Franklin wanted more equipment to conduct experiments. He hired a glassblower and silversmith to make him new gadgets. He acquired a special piece of equipment called an **electrostatic machine** to help with his research. He also got his Junto buddies to take part in various experiments. Franklin focused on static electricity in several of his electrical experiments.

STORING CHARGES & BIG DISCOVERIES

Ben Franklin had equipment to generate static electricity. But he also wanted to be able to collect an electrical charge so he could study its properties more carefully. A new invention called the **Leyden jar** made this much more feasible.

What Is the Electrostatic Machine?

A blown glass globe or sphere rests on top of a wooden base padded in leather. The globe is attached to a small wooden wheel. A thin iron rod goes through both the glass globe and the small wooden wheel to keep them in place. Underneath the globe is a large wooden wheel, mounted vertically with a handle at the end for turning. A leather strap around the large wheel's rim connects it to both the glass globe and the smaller wheel above. When someone turns the larger wheel, the smaller wheel also spins, which makes the glass globe spin. As a result, friction is created between the globe and the leather pad underneath it. This produces a static electrical charge inside the globe. When someone touches a metal point (or a set of points) to the glass, that point draws off the electrical charge.

Invented in 1745 , a Leyden jar is a storage container for electricity. Its earliest version consisted of a glass jar coated inside and outside with metal foil. Water filled the inside of the Leyden jar and a wire ran from the foil coating inside the jar out the top. This invention was essential to the early study of electricity because it was the first device that could store an electrical charge to be used later.

Leyden jars

No one could ever say that Ben Franklin was all work and no play. Once he'd acquired his Leyden jars, he engaged in some funny experimentation. He made a metal spider and applied an electrical charge to it so it moved like a real one. He also rigged a portrait of England's King George II (1683–1760) that would shock anyone who touched his golden crown. Ha!

WORDS TO KNOW

electron: a particle in an atom with a negative charge that moves around the nucleus.

nucleus: the center of an atom, made up of protons and neutrons. The plural is nuclei.

proton: a particle in the nucleus of an atom that has a positive charge.

neutron: a particle in the nucleus of an atom that has no charge.

single-fluid theory of electricity: the theory that electricity flows both within and between objects and that an excess of fluid makes some objects positive, while a lack of fluid makes others negative.

Could people pass electricity to one another? Franklin wanted to know. He asked a few others to draw charges from the electrostatic machine and then touch each other. Did sparks fly? Yes!

Franklin learned a lot from this experiment. He discovered that it is possible for a static electrical charge to pass, or flow, from one individual to another by touching. He also found out that electricity doesn't disappear or vanish, though it does move from one person or object to another.

Understanding Electricity

Electricity is a form of energy. It can power items from televisions to ovens. But what causes electrical energy? Tiny particles called **electrons**. Everything in the universe is made up of atoms. In the center of every atom is a **nucleus**. The nucleus contains **protons**, which have a positive electrical charge, and **neutrons**, which have no charge. Smaller particles called electrons spin around the nucleus. These electrons have a negative electrical charge. Opposite electrical charges—the positive charges and the negative charges—attract each other, so the electrons move around from atom to atom as the charges work to balance out. It is this movement of electrons between atoms that causes electrical energy.

Some objects can conduct electricity—that is, they allow electricity to easily flow through them. We call these conductors. Metal objects such as coins, paperclips, and silverware are all good conductors. Electricity does not flow easily though other materials. We call these insulators. Paper, rubber, and some kinds of plastics are examples of insulators. Remember your experiments with insulators?

So, what happens when two objects are rubbed together with the goal of collecting static electricity? Using Franklin's terms—still in use in the 2020s—a positive charge passes into one object, while a negative charge goes into the other one.

Is the positive charge bigger than the negative one? No, they are always the same. A spark or a shock shows how the energy is moving as the two types of charges equalize.

Based on his experiments, Benjamin Franklin figured out that two different kinds of fluids did not make up electricity. Instead, he came up with what's known as the **single-fluid theory of electricity**.

Uncertainty

Scientists are not always confident about their work. Even the great Ben Franklin had doubts about where his research into electricity was going. In late April 1749, he wrote a letter to a friend expressing some frustration. He had revised his theories and even experienced a couple of painful electrical shocks. As a result of these experiences, Franklin went so far as to declare that the only use for electricity was that "it may make a vain man humble."

WORDS TO KNOW

conservation of charge: the scientific concept that electricity has equal amounts of positive and negative charges.

Another very important discovery was that electricity has equal amounts of positive and negative charges. This is now called the **conservation of charge**.

Even the Leyden jars themselves captured Ben Franklin's interest. He experimented with them by dumping the water out of a Leyden jar. He discovered that it wasn't the water that was holding the electrical charge.

Glass is an insulator and foil is a conductor. It was the glass jar itself that held the charge. Franklin used this information to create something new—the first electric battery. He lined up a row of several glass plates. These plates were surrounded by metal and wired together. The device—and the term "battery"—were Franklin's inventions. As time passed, he refined the battery's design and increased the amount of electrical charge that could be produced by a battery made of multiple Leyden jars. Smart!

Ben Franklin came up with the term "ELECTRICIAN," which he used to refer to scientists such as himself who experimented with electricity.

A CHANGE OF VENUE & ONE WILD PARTY

Benjamin Franklin commonly started his experiments in indoor spaces and then moved them outdoors, into the wider natural world. That's what he did with his electricity experimentation.

In the summer of 1749, Franklin thought it might be fun to have a party on the banks of Philadelphia's Schuylkill River. Franklin described the party in true scientific fashion: "A turkey is to be killed for our dinners by the electrical shock; and roasted by the electrical jack, before a fire kindled by the electrified bottle; while the health of all the famous electricians in England, France, and Germany are to be drank in electrified bumpers, under the discharge of guns from the electrical battery."

Franklin's bash was a blast—literally! Even though a turkey was harder to kill by electric shock than chickens (which he had already done successfully), Franklin and his buddies eventually succeeded in zapping the turkey by linking together a large battery that provided enough charge to kill it. Franklin described the meat of the fried turkey as "uncommonly tender."

Benjamin Franklin created the first electrical battery. **Read about his creation here.** How does the battery he made differ from those we use today? Which do you think keeps its charge longer or has more power?

🔎 "Electrical battery" of Leyden jars

PS

Electricity and the Human Body

People sometimes say, "Electricity is everywhere." Electrical energy is even *inside* your body. The cells of the human body are specially designed to be able to conduct electrical currents. For example, the nervous system needs electricity to send signals through the body to the brain. This makes many essential bodily functions possible—from thinking and feeling to moving.

There's a bundle of nerves in a person's heart that function like an electric power plant. When electricity goes through the heart, it causes the muscle cells to contract. An electrocardiogram (also called ECG or EKG) is a test that measures the heart's electrical activity. You might have seen one when watching TV or a movie—a wavy line across a display screen moves, showing the electrical pulses in the heart. (If the line goes flat, the person's heart is not working and they are dying.) An ECG can show how fast a person's heart is beating, the rhythm of their heartbeats, and the timing of each of the heart's chambers as they squeeze.

Have you ever heard of a pacemaker? This amazing device is a lifesaver for people whose hearts do not work properly. A pacemaker is able to send out electrical impulses that stimulate the heart so that it keeps beating normally.

LIGHTNING & LETTERS

Were there any potential similarities between lightning and electricity? Ben Franklin wanted to know. Perhaps Franklin became curious about lightning when he witnessed thunderstorms over the Delaware River during the summer of 1749. He had also read official reports from other colonies of the damage thunderstorms caused to homes, trees, people, and more. He knew from firsthand experience as a firefighter in Philadelphia the extent of the damage that lightning strikes could do to homes, even on the inside.

In November 1749, Franklin wrote down a dozen similarities between electrical sparks and lightning in his science journal. Here are some:

- giving light
- color of the light
- swift motion
- crooked directions
- being conducted by metals
- crack or noise in exploding
- melting metals
- destroying animals
- sulfurous smell

This list helped him think more about lightning and electricity and how they were connected.

Benjamin Franklin wrote down many of his ideas about electricity in letters to friends living in England. He explained the details of his various experiments involving electricity, as well as

Dr. John Fothergill (1712–1780) of London's Royal Society praised Franklin's work on electricity, saying that Franklin "has said more sensible things on the subject and let us see more into the nature of this delicate affair than all the other writers put together." **You can read *Experiments* yourself at this website.**

🔍 Archives Franklin experiments electricity

PS

other ideas and theories he had on the subject. In 1751, these writings were collected and published in a short book called *Experiments And Observations On Electricity, Made At Philadelphia in America.*

Electrifying!

Being a scientist is dangerous work. On Christmas 1750, Franklin tried to **electrocute** a turkey and received a violent electric shock when he was accidentally jolted by two nearly fully charged large Leyden jars. Ever the scientist, he wrote about the sensations he experienced when the shock went through both his arms and body. He described his senses as being gone—he didn't see or hear the shock that went through him even though the flash was bright and the noise loud. He also developed a round swelling on his hand where the shock hit it and his breastbone felt bruised for about a week after the event. Ouch!

 You can read about the event in his own words at this website.

🔎 Mass hist Franklin turkey

Benjamin Franklin's new book on electricity was a huge success. It was soon translated into French, German, Italian, and even Latin. Through his writing, Benjamin Franklin greatly expanded the world's understanding of electricity. It made Franklin famous around the world. And that was before his most famous experiment ever.

Franklin wanted to prove that lightning was electricity in true scientific fashion, through observation and **analysis**. But his plan needed a hill or a tall building, neither of which Philadelphia had at the time. Did he stop experimenting just because there wasn't such a building yet? No. Instead, he worked on another plan—one that involved a kite and a key.

Franklin wrote a series of letters describing what might happen to a man standing on a box next to a metal rod during a storm. THESE LETTERS WERE FAMOUS in France even before Franklin performed his kite experiment.

WORDS TO KNOW

lightning rod: a metal rod attached to the highest point of a building that attracts lightning and guides it to the ground.

One afternoon in June 1752, the sky grew dark over Philadelphia. Ben Franklin had been waiting for a thunderstorm—he was excited and prepared. He had made a kite from a silk handkerchief so it would be able to tolerate the winds and rain. The kite had a sharp wire, or rod, attached to the top of its frame. This tiny metal rod stuck out so that it could conduct electricity. In Franklin's words, he thought the rod would "draw fire from the clouds."

Franklin attached a hemp string to the bottom of his strange-looking kite and then a silk string to that. Why two different strings? If the hemp string got rained on, it would easily conduct an electrical charge, since water is a conductor. The silk one, which was intended to stay dry (with Franklin standing under a shed holding it), would not. Franklin attached a metal key between the hemp string and the silk string. Lastly, he ran a piece of thin wire from the key to the top of a Leyden jar.

Credit: Alfred Jones, for the Bureau of Engraving and Printing

Franklin's son William helped him get the kite aloft. After a while, Franklin saw that the loose threads on the hemp string were standing erect. He then touched his knuckle to the key and felt an electric spark.

Lightning did not actually strike Franklin's kite. Instead, the kite came into contact with tiny amounts of electricity collecting inside the storm clouds. But Franklin was able to collect "electric fire very copiously" with his Leyden jar. He found that the charge he collected in the Leyden jar demonstrated the same qualities as the electricity he had produced in a laboratory setting. His experiment was a success!

FRANKLIN'S LIGHTNING ROD

Franklin now knew that lightning and electricity were the same. Plus, he found a practical use for what he'd learned.

Back then, many houses burned down after being struck by lightning. Franklin also knew that lightning typically hit the highest point of a building. He worked on an invention that would help solve this problem.

Sometimes, inspiration comes in the form of an everyday item. During earlier experiments, he found that knitting needles could draw off a discharge of electricity from his electrostatic machine. He would use these sharp needles to transfer the charge to be stored in his Leyden jar. Franklin wondered whether this type of design could be used on a bigger scale to help deal with lightning strikes. Thus, the **lightning rod** was invented.

"May not the knowledge of the **POWER OF POINTS** be of use to mankind, in preserving houses, churches, ships, etc., from the stroke of lightning, by directing us to fix, on the highest parts of those edifices, upright rods of iron made **SHARP AS A NEEDLE** . . . . Would not these pointed rods probably draw the electrical fire silently out of a cloud before it came night enough to strike, and thereby secure us from that most sudden and **TERRIBLE MISCHIEF!**"

—Ben Franklin

WORDS TO KNOW

electrical current: the flow of electrons through a material.

advocate: to publicly support.

blunt: having a rounded or flat end.

prestigious: inspiring respect and admiration.

How does a lightning rod work? A pointed metal rod is attached to a building's roof. The rod is connected to a wire that runs down the outside of the building and into the ground. The lightning rod works by conducting the huge, harmful **electrical currents** found in lightning away from the building and into the ground, where they won't cause damage, since soil is not a good conductor.

The first lightning rods were installed in Philadelphia during the summer of 1752. Franklin installed one on his own house as well. Did this invention work? You bet! Before long, lightning rods became normal fixtures on buildings all over the American colonies.

An illustration from *A Comic History of the United States*, 1880

No Lightning Rods, Please!

Not all people thought lightning rods were a good idea. Lots of people in Franklin's era thought that lightning was a sign of God's anger. They believed it was wrong to get in the way of this sign. Some folks also wondered whether directing lightning into the ground could cause earthquakes. When an earthquake hit Boston in 1755, some locals believed that lightning rods were to blame for the quake.

Of all his many inventions, Ben Franklin thought his lightning rod was the most important.

It might seem that all lightning rods looked exactly the same. But that wasn't the case. Franklin was an **advocate** for lightning rods with sharp points. However, his colleagues from England disagreed. They believed sharp rods attracted lightning and therefore increased the risk of being struck by lightning. They preferred lightning rods with **blunt** tips.

In 1753, Franklin received the prestigious COPLEY MEDAL from the Royal Society in recognition of his "CURIOUS EXPERIMENTS and observations on electricity."

What did King George choose for his palace? A blunt rod—he was English. In the colonies, people supported Franklin's ideas about how to protect their public buildings and chose pointed lightning rods. But the English felt choosing pointed rods showed disobedience to the king.

Whose lightning rod choice was better? That depends who you ask. A 1983 *New York Times* article discusses research that showed lightning rods with blunt tips more effectively route lightning to the ground in a harmless way. But in 2016, lightning struck the Maryland State House's pointed (and centuries-old) lightning rod, saving it from destruction.

ESSENTIAL QUESTION

How did Ben Franklin change peoples' understanding of electricity?

MAKE A
LEYDEN JAR

The invention of the Leyden jar allowed Ben Franklin to advance his experiments with electricity. Make your own Leyden jar and have a friend or family member test it out. Don't worry—the shock will be very minor, similar to touching a doorknob after walking across a rug.

> **Use the hammer to gently tap the nail through the cap of your bottled water.** Be sure to leave the head of the nail sticking out a bit from the cap—don't hammer it flat against the cap.

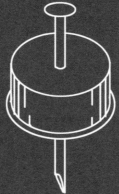

> **Starting 2 or 3 inches below the cap of the bottle, wrap a layer of aluminum foil around the outside of the bottle.** Try to keep the foil smooth and tightly connected to the bottle. You should be able to see inside the bottle.

> **Use a rubber band or two to secure the foil in place against the outside of the bottle.** Your Leyden jar is done!

> **Have your helper hold the Leyden jar, gripping it by its aluminum foil layer.**

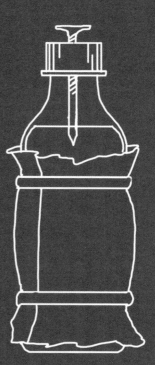

TEXT TO **WORLD**

How might the world be different without Franklin's electricity experiments?

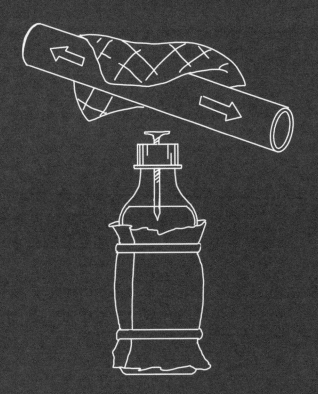

At the same time, charge the Leyden jar. In one hand, take hold of the acrylic tube. Rub a clean cotton cloth or paper towel against the tube. Keep sliding the cloth up and down the whole length of the tube until you hear a crackling sound or feel the static charge. Continue to slide the paper towel or cloth against the tube while you slide the tube against the nail that is sticking out of the cap. What happens if you touch the nail now?

Think Like Ben!

Get a few more people to help. Have the person holding the Leyden jar in one hand also hold hands with another group member. All group members should hold hands in a chain. What happens when one person touches the nail?

Jean-Antoine Nollet

A French physicist and priest named Jean-Antoine Nollet (1700–1770) took what people today would say were unsafe risks when experimenting with Leyden jars. One time he used Leyden jars to give an electrical shock to 180 French soldiers. Why? As a form of entertainment for a king! Another time, he had 700 monks join in a circle connected to a Leyden jar. Electricity traveled through the human chain. Were these experiments dangerous? Absolutely. But they also showed how quickly the electricity traveled from person to person. Today, scientists typically must get permission to use other people as part of their experimentation.

CRAZY
CEREAL

CACHE KIT
- plastic or hard rubber comb
- tiny pieces of dry cereal, such as Cheerios
- 12-inch-long piece of thread
- tape
- hair or a wool sweater

Many of Ben Franklin's experiments focused on static electricity. Try this one involving a comb and some cereal.

❯ **Wash the comb and dry it thoroughly.**

❯ **Tie one piece of the cereal to one end of your piece of thread.** Use tape to attach the other end of the thread to the edge of a chair or table so that it can hang freely and not touch anything.

❯ **Run the comb through your (dry) hair several times to charge it.** If you don't have longish hair, find a person who does. You can also rub the comb against a wool sweater several times instead.

❯ **Slowly bring the comb close to the cereal.** What happens? Keep the comb still until the cereal seems to jump away on its own.

❯ **Touch the comb again to the cereal.** What happens?

Think Like Ben!

Repeat the experiment using a balloon instead of a comb. How did the results of the comb versus balloon differ, if at all?

WHAT'S HAPPENING?

When you combed your hair, electrons moved from your hair to the comb and gave the comb a negative charge of static electricity. The cereal, which was neutral, was attracted to the comb. When the comb and cereal touched, electrons shifted slowly from the comb to the cereal. Once both objects had a negative charge, the cereal was repelled by the comb.

LIGHT IT UP!

Can you get any light from a light bulb using only a balloon? Try this activity to find out!

Caution: Do not use electricity from an outlet for this activity.

❯ **Blow up your balloon and tie it off.**

❯ **Bring the balloon and the light bulb into a dark room.**

❯ **Rub the balloon against your hair or the wool sweater many times.** It's helpful to build up a lot of static electricity for this experiment.

❯ **Touch the charged part of the balloon to your light bulb.** Pay close attention—watch the bulb carefully. What do you see? What happens when you touch different parts of the light bulb?

Think Like Ben!

Instead of trying to light up a bulb with a static-charged balloon, see what happens when you try to move an aluminum can using the same balloon. Tip: Put the can onto its side so it rolls easier. How far can you make the can move, if at all? You can also try moving a ping-pong ball instead of a can. Another idea is to see which materials are attracted to the balloon after you've rubbed it against your hair or the wool sweater. Try some of the following: packing peanuts, small pieces of aluminum foil, string, and confetti.

Chapter 4

HOME IS WHERE DESIGN
HAPPENS

THE NEWSPAPER ALWAYS ENDS UP IN MY PARENTS' BUSHES, SO I USED THIS TO REACH IT.

NOW THIS LOOKS FAMILIAR! I INVENTED A SIMILAR DEVICE TO HELP REACH BOOKS ON THE SHELVES IN MY HOME.

FROM WHAT I READ, YOU LOVED MAKING THINGS TO IMPROVE YOUR HOME LIFE.

YES! AND AS I LIKE TO SAY, NECESSITY IS THE MOTHER OF INVENTION.

Even though Benjamin Franklin was a world-class scientist, he also was a practical man who loved making improvements to his home. From construction ideas to furniture design, Franklin used science and innovation to make his dwellings more comfortable and manageable.

ESSENTIAL QUESTION

How was Franklin an example of the quote, "Necessity is the mother of invention?"

In November 1762, Ben Franklin returned from seven years working in London. He felt it was time to build a new home of his own in Philadelphia.

The house was still under construction when Franklin's work took him back to London. So his wife, Deborah, had to oversee the construction. Did that stop Franklin from expressing his preferences and building ideas? Absolutely not!

Franklin's letters to his wife about the new house—and her responses—offer extraordinary detail about its construction and **embellishment**. He requested **technical** details about his new house, from room dimensions to color schemes so he could order items such as carpets and curtains while in Europe. Not only did he purchase fabric, but he gave very specific directions for how he wanted the curtains made and hung. Sadly, Franklin didn't see his new house until 1775, by which point Deborah had passed away.

House Size Through American History

When Benjamin Franklin's home was built in the 1760s, it had nine rooms. This was an absolute mansion compared to an average Colonial American house. At that time, most families lived in one-room houses, while wealthier folks might have four rooms—two upstairs and two downstairs. Although an average American household in 1790 had 5.79 people, in 2010 that figure had dropped to just 2.58 people. And yet 81 percent of new homes built in 2018 had three or more bedrooms. Why do you think homes are getting bigger even though a smaller number of people are living in them?

Despite the fancy furniture he chose and the music room that housed his armonica and many other instruments, Ben Franklin didn't get to enjoy his new house for long. He was only home from May 1775 until October 1776, when he headed out for a long political assignment in France.

Founding Father Franklin came home from his last overseas assignment in 1785. But the great scientist and collector decided he had too many possessions to fit in his relatively new house. Not to mention his daughter Sally, son-in-law Richard Basse, and their seven children were now living there, too. What did he do? Build an addition!

Franklin was excited about being able to witness the construction and supervise any details that needed to be looked over.

WORDS TO KNOW

long arm: a mechanical arm invented by Ben Franklin that was used to reach books on high shelves.

arthritis: a medical condition that causes swollen joints, stiffness, and pain.

The house that Benjamin Franklin designed was torn down in 1812. In its place, a new street and a number of smaller houses were built. But you can see the outline of where the house stood at the Franklin Court site.

REACHING THOSE BOOKS!

Ben Franklin loved to read, so, perhaps not surprisingly, he invented a special piece of furniture that helped with this hobby. Sometime between 1760 and 1780, Franklin invented what is now known as his library chair. One side of Franklin's chair had a seat for sitting, but when the seat was turned over, a small step ladder was revealed. After Franklin was done with a book, he could flip the seat over, climb the stepladder, and put the book back on the shelf—even a relatively high shelf. Clever!

"I hardly know how to justify building a **LIBRARY AT AN AGE** that will so soon **oblige me to quit it; but we are apt to** forget that we are grown old, and Building is an Amusement."
—Benjamin Franklin

In his old age, Benjamin Franklin didn't feel safe climbing up steps to get his books off the high shelves. So, what did he do? In 1786, he came up with the **long arm**, designed to reach books located on high shelves. It had two finger-like grippers attached to the end of a pipe or piece of wood. You opened or closed the grippers by pulling on a cord.

Franklin was quite proud of this handy invention. He wrote up a super-detailed description of the long arm. Drawings? Check. Diagrams? Check. His writings on the long arm also included tips for how to build it—right down to the 8-foot-long piece of wood, the size of the wood screws he used, and the width of the cord to pull the grippers closed.

When Franklin died in 1790, he owned about 4,276 BOOKS. His grandson William Temple Franklin (1760–1823) sold many of them after Franklin's death.

Franklin was also pleased that, unlike many other new tools, the long arm was easy to master.

Are long arms still in use? You bet! They are not often seen in libraries, but cleanup crews often use stainless steel versions of Franklin's long arm to pick up trash along highways. Some folks who have **arthritis** use similar devices to reduce the strain on their joints when gripping objects. Long arms can also be helpful for adults who are shorter than average.

FUN WITH FURNITURE

Some say that Ben Franklin invented the rocking chair in the 1760s. But that's definitely not true. Rocking chairs were around for years before Franklin put his own spin on what some have called "an American invention." A number of experts believe the rocking chair was invented in New England around 1740.

One adaptation that Franklin made to the rocking chair involved a fan. He attached a foot pedal to his rocking chair that was connected to an overhead fan made from a **palmetto** leaf. While relaxing in his chair, Franklin could also stay cool! Another perk? This fan shooed away flies.

Another adaptation Franklin made to a rocking chair was connecting it to a **butter churn**. As the person in the chair rocked, the rocking motion powered a butter churn! Super efficient!

ROCKING CHAIRS have been designed for other tasks, such as stirring moonshine and keeping bugs away. Several versions of rocking chairs were even touted as preventing disease.

We can't be certain what Franklin's creation looked like because no drawings or photographs of his rocking chair butter churn exist. But in 1913, an inventor by the name of Alfred Clark applied for a patent for his rocking chair butter churn. In his version, the rocking chair was attached to a barrel churn. As the rocking chair moved, so did the barrel, and the milk was churned into butter. Perhaps Clark was inspired by Franklin's ingenuity.

Thomas Jefferson and Furniture

If you've ever sat in a swivel chair, you know how much fun it can be to spin around and around. Founding Father Thomas Jefferson (1743–1826) invented the swivel chair. Like Franklin, Jefferson dabbled in furniture invention. He added a swivel mechanism to his Windsor chair to create the type of spinning chair found in offices all over the world today. Jefferson might have invented another interesting kind of chair. Have you ever sat in a classroom at a chair with a partial desk attached to it? There is some debate about who created such a writing chair. Some sources say it was Benjamin Franklin. But many others think it was Thomas Jefferson who added a writing surface onto one arm of a Windsor chair. Perhaps this was where Jefferson drafted the Declaration of Independence . . . but there are debates about this, too! What does this tell you about history?

A TIMELY INVENTION

Most homes today have some type of clock. Perhaps it's a digital clock built into the microwave or a fancy grandfather clock. During his time in London, probably around the year 1758, Benjamin Franklin invented a new kind of clock, with three wheels. Historians think he created this clock out of a desire to make a simpler clock.

One thing is odd about this invention. Unlike with most of his creations, Franklin doesn't seem to have written any description of it. Throughout his life, Franklin tended to write detailed notes and make sketches to share his thought processes and techniques for any scientific endeavor he embarked on.

Watch Ben Franklin's clock working here.

🔎 Benjamin Franklin's Clock Movement Design

So, how do we know anything about Franklin's three-wheel clock? An instrument maker and scientist named James Ferguson (1710–1776) wrote about it in detail in a book called *Select Mechanical Exercises*, published in 1773.

IS THAT A CLOCK, BY SOME CHANCE?

YES. IT IS CALLED A DIGITAL CLOCK.

I MUST SAY, IT'S SO MUCH SIMPLER THAN THE CLOCK I DESIGNED.

WORDS TO KNOW

concentric: having a common center.

pulley: a simple machine consisting of a wheel with a grooved rim that a rope or chain is pulled through to help lift a load.

work: the amount of energy needed to move an object a certain distance.

Franklin's three-wheel clock looked very different from the clocks in use today. It had two faces. The smaller face was on the top of the clock and showed the seconds. The larger face was on the bottom of the clock. It featured three **concentric** circles, each of which was divided into four quarters.

Sixty individual minutes were marked on each quarter, with big numerals showing 10-minute increments—10, 20, 30, 40, 50, 60. What was strange about this clock is that the big face had only one hand and it took just four hours for this hand to travel around the entire dial. Clocks today have both hour and minute hands, and it takes 12 hours for the hour hand to travel around the dial.

Someone looking at Franklin's three-wheel clock would need to have some idea of the time. After all, the hand could be on hour I at the same time as hours V and IX. Today, we'd consider it confusing. But Franklin would disagree. His clock was considered simpler than others of the period.

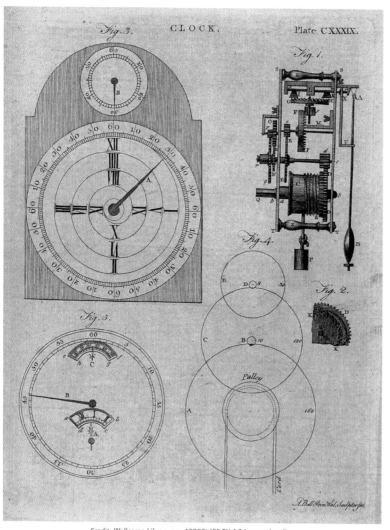

Credit: Wellcome Library no. 40898i (CC BY 4.0 International)

OTHER HOME IMPROVEMENTS

Have you ever been in bed, heard somebody knock, and wished you could open the door without getting out from under your cozy blankets? Well, Ben Franklin might have had the solution.

Near the very end of his life, Franklin was in a lot of pain and was bedridden. Although not mentioned in most biographies about the great inventor, a number of sources say that he invented a **pulley** system that allowed him to both unlock and lock his bedroom door from the comfort of his bed. We don't have any pictures or even sketches of Franklin's bedroom pulley system. We do understand, however, how pulleys work in general.

Create your own pulley!
Visit this website for simple instructions.

🔎 wikihow build pulley

PS

Pulleys in Action

Pulleys are a way to redirect force. They are often used by people who need to move a very heavy object. Is it easier to pull up on a heavy object or pull down? With a pulley, you can change the direction of the force you are using. That's how flags are run up flagpoles—a pulley at the top lets you pull a rope down from the top of the flagpole and the flag goes up! A pulley also gives you a mechanical advantage by increasing the amount of force you produce, even when performing the same amount of **work**. The more rope you add to your system, the less force you need to exert to do the heavy lifting.

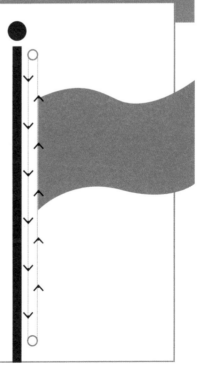

Ben Franklin's system must have involved some kind of pulley through which he could pull a rope while still in bed. The rope must have been connected to the door handle. The force Ben exerted by pulling the rope would cause the door handle to turn and unlock the door.

"Several clocks have been made according to this **INGENIOUS PLAN** of the Doctor's [Franklin's], and I can affirm, that I have seen one of them **which measures time exceedingly well. The simpler that any machine** is, the better it will be allowed to be, by every **MAN OF SCIENCE.**" —James Ferguson, scientist

Some sources claim that Benjamin Franklin invented something called the "busybody." Others say that Franklin came across this device when serving as an **ambassador** to France. This clever creation consisted of three mirrors that were positioned in such a way that the elderly scientist could catch a view of visitors at his front door—all without having to get up.

How does a busybody work? Three mirrors are placed on a pole or rod from a second (or third) floor window. The mirrors are put at different angles so that somebody inside can see the street underneath that window. Modern versions are still sold and attached to windowsills with screws.

From furniture to the long arm, Ben Franklin came up with many devices that made his home life easier. Visitors to Franklin's home often wrote about the wide variety of "useful curiosities" they saw there.

While Franklin thought of many things to help around his own house and community, his mind kept working as he traveled. Let's take a look at some of the innovations and experiments he did while far from home.

ESSENTIAL QUESTION

How was Franklin an example of the quote, "Necessity is the mother of invention?"

MULTITASKING
FURNITURE

Ben Franklin's library chair could be used for sitting but also as a stepladder. Some footstools today also act as storage spaces for clutter. And some highchairs can convert into booster seats or even adult-sized chairs. In this activity, you'll design and create a model of a piece of furniture that serves its original purpose but also does something else.

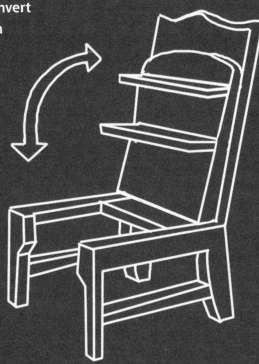

❯ **Walk around your home and look at all the different types of furniture.** Think about which ones would be the easiest to adapt or change so that they could be used for an additional purpose.

❯ **Brainstorm and list a few ideas for multipurpose furniture.** No idea is too out there!

❯ **Choose your favorite idea and sketch it out in your science journal.** If the new piece of furniture results in a different shape, be sure to show how it looks before and after its conversion.

❯ **Create a miniature model of your new furniture design.** Did it work well? If not, what can you change so it is easier to use?

Think Like Ben!

An inexpensive way to change the look and functionality of a room can be to rearrange furniture. Can you draw a sketch of a room in your home in which you shift things around to make it more functional? attractive? user-friendly?

TEXT TO **WORLD**

What might Franklin have thought about the technology we use today to keep our homes secure? Do you think he would have thought about ways to improve on alarms, cameras, and electric gates?

HOW BIG IS YOUR
DREAM HOME?

When Benjamin Franklin built his home off Market Street in Philadelphia, he wanted many things—bedrooms, a kitchen, a music room, a library, and so on. What would your dream house include? How big would it be?

❯ In your science journal, list all the features of your dream house—the number of bedrooms, bathrooms, and other spaces you'd like to have.

❯ Create a **blueprint** by sketching out the shapes and rough sizes of the various rooms.

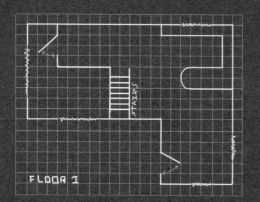

❯ Before you decide how big the rooms should be, see how big each room is where you live now. Measure the length and width (in feet) of each room. Then, calculate the square footage of a room by multiplying the length by the width. If a room is 12 feet by 10 feet, its square footage is 120 square feet. Use this information to decide on the square footage of rooms in your dream house.

In 2018, the **median** square footage that an American home buyer wanted was 2,066 square feet. Do some research to find out the average house size in other countries. How do American homes compare to those around the world?

WORDS TO KNOW

blueprint: a model or template to follow.

median: the middle value in a list of numbers.

SECTION LOOKING EAST

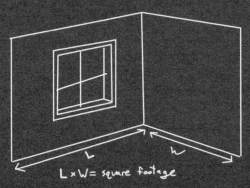

L x W = square footage

❯ **Add up the square footages of each room to get the total area of your house.**

❯ **Use a sheet of graph paper and create a blueprint of your dream home.** Make it to scale. Each square on the grid could represent a certain measurement. For example, each square might be 2 or 4 feet.

Think Like Ben!

The average apartment in the United States is about 882 square feet. What would your ideal apartment design look like if yours was this size? Create a blueprint showing the various rooms and their square footages.

GRAB IT!

Ben Franklin designed a very sturdy grabber to pick up heavy objects such as books. You can build your own to pick up lighter objects.

❯ **To build your grabber's handle, place your paint stirrers so that one overlaps the other by about 4 inches.** Use a couple of strips of tape to cover the area where they overlap. You now should have one very long stick.

❯ **Cut four strips of cardboard, each measuring 10 inches long by 1½ inches wide.** You might find it easier to first score the cardboard using the open blade of the scissors and then cut all the way through. Ask an adult to help you do this! Cut one of the 10-inch strips in half so you have two 5-inch strips.

❯ **To make hinge holes in your cardboard, use the sharpened pencil.** Put the holes in the locations shown on the illustration. Be careful not to make the holes too large and to keep them at least ½ inch from the cardboard's edges.

❯ **Take the strip of cardboard without any holes.** Fold it in half lengthwise. Use your ruler to measure and mark 1 inch from the fold. Use your pencil to poke a hole in the middle of the last inch of cardboard. Diagram A shows how the other 4 inches of this cardboard should overlap with the wooden stick handle beneath it. Tape this cardboard to the handle.

CACHE KIT
- wooden paint stirrers
- masking or packing tape
- cardboard
- ruler
- pencil with sharpened end
- 4 metal fasteners, 1½ inches long
- a rubber band (ideally about ⅛ inch by 3½ inches in size)
- string
- foam, paperclips, craft sticks, or other materials to improve the grabber's grip
- variety of objects to pick up

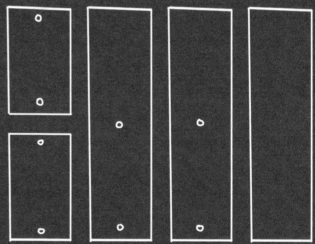

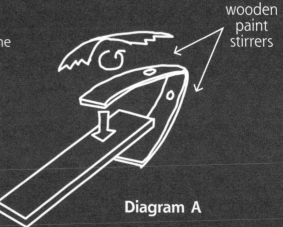

wooden paint stirrers

Diagram A

> **Make an X out of the two 10-inch pieces of cardboard that have holes in the center.** Place a metal fastener through the central holes of both pieces. It should look like the X in Diagram B. Before closing this fastener, place it through the hole in the cardboard at the end of the handle.

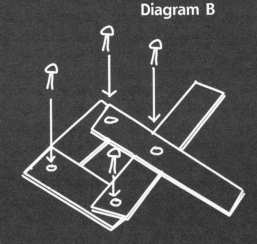

Diagram B

> **Now take the two 5-inch strips of cardboard and attach them to the ends of the X you just made.** For each 5-inch strip, place a fastener through it and also through the hole at one end of the cardboard X. Finally, place a fastener through the holes at the very end of the 5-inch cardboard segments. You can see how this looks in Diagram B.

> **Be sure all your fastener tabs are completely flat and taped down.** Stretch the rubber band, placing one end under the top of one of the middle fasteners and the other end under the top of the other middle fastener, as shown in Diagram C. Tie a piece of string to the end of the rubber band that is closest to the handle. The string should be a couple of inches longer than the handle itself.

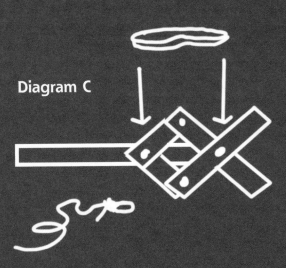

Diagram C

> **Try out your grabber by pulling the string.** Can you grab some objects with it? Do you have any trouble grabbing certain objects?

> **Use foam, craft sticks, or other available materials to see if you can improve how well your grabber grips.**

Think Like Ben!

Can you easily pick up objects such as a cup, a pen, or a ball with your grabber? Can you catch something with it?

Chapter 5

MAILINGS &
MAPS

Ben Franklin did a lot to improve his own home and the town of Philadelphia, and he traveled so much that it made sense for him to apply that scientific curiosity wherever he went. Whether he was finding the best way to deliver mail to the next town over or figuring out the fastest way to travel from America to Europe, Franklin was insatiable when it came to new knowledge.

Let's rewind a few centuries to find out more about mail and mapping, and what Ben Franklin had to do with them.

ESSENTIAL QUESTION

What do you think Benjamin Franklin would think about traveling in airplanes?

In the earliest times, the American colonies had no regular mail service and no post offices. So, how did mail get sent? Some colonists paid travelers to carry their letters. Others asked **merchant** ships to transport their mail. Colonists might also pick up their mail at a local **tavern.**

In those days, the mail wasn't very reliable. Letters were easily lost or stolen. The mail routes varied quite a bit because they were operated locally rather than by a **centralized** mail service. Mail traveled by boat from Europe to the colonies and by riders on horseback within the colonies. A letter could take many weeks to get to its destination!

In the decade leading up to 2018, the number of FIRST-CLASS MAIL items sent by the U.S. Postal Service dropped by MORE THAN HALF. Why might this be?

Benjamin Franklin was a constant letter writer. And in 1737, his postal career began. That year, he became the **postmaster general** of Philadelphia. In 1753, he became **deputy** postmaster general for the colonies. This was the most prestigious postal job in all of America!

News Diet

Today, thanks to the internet, people around the globe get an almost instant stream of news in real time. It's pretty easy to keep up with important events. But back in Franklin's day, information did not travel quickly. For example, the full text of the Declaration of Independence was printed in the *Pennsylvania Evening Post* on July 6, 1776. This text spread slowly from Philadelphia through the colonies. It wasn't until August 2 that a South Carolina newspaper published the text. This meant it was harder to be an informed citizen in Franklin's day. Today, a media organization publishes an online story and the headlines get emailed, texted, and posted on social media within seconds. Almost immediately, people around the world begin to offer their reactions and opinions to the news! Do you think this process is better or worse? Why? What effect might that immediacy have on people's attention spans, mental health, and democracy?

WORDS TO KNOW

ford: a shallow place in a stream or river that allows people to drive or walk across.

Franklin treated his postmaster jobs just like any other scientific endeavor—with organization and attention to detail. He came up with detailed procedures for running the postal service efficiently. For example, in 1743, he criticized the way that people had to crowd onto ships in search of their letters. Instead, he suggested, ship captains have all the packages and letters delivered to a post office, where clerks could sort and distribute everything properly. Franklin also established the dead letter office, a place where undeliverable mail could go.

Benjamin Franklin wrote or received more than 15,000 LETTERS during his lifetime.

It was under Franklin's watch that home delivery of mail began. The next time you get a nice card in the mail, perhaps you should thank Ben Franklin!

The B. Free Franklin post office in Philadelphia, the only Colonial post office still open for business.

Credit: Jeremy Thompson (CC BY 2.0)

MAPPING THE MAIL

If you wanted to travel to a destination far away, how would you figure out the most efficient route? Many people would use a mapping app such as Google Maps. How did mail carriers in the American colonies find the quickest ways to transport letters from point A to point B?

During Colonial times, the person RECEIVING a letter had to pay the postage, not the person SENDING it.

Here's where Ben Franklin comes in. One of his goals as postmaster was to set up more efficient mail routes. In 1753, he traveled along the Boston Post Road, the earliest postal route connecting Boston and New York City. In 1754, Franklin traveled to all the northern colonies' post offices. And between 1755 and 1756, he visited the ones in Maryland and Virginia. During these trips, Franklin surveyed the land. He was looking for the best roads, **fords**, or ferries to help postal carriers get the mail where it needed to go—quickly.

A painting of Ben Franklin on the Boston Post Road

Credit: Carl Rakeman, 1878–1965

WORDS TO KNOW

odometer: a device that measures the distance traveled, especially by a vehicle.

profitable: making money from a business or activity.

Franklin didn't have a smartphone with a mapping app, but he was very capable of following a paper map.

In 1763, Franklin went on yet another tour to inspect post offices in New England and all the way down to Virginia, surveying the land at the same time. Unfortunately, this tour was interrupted when Franklin was hurt after falling from a horse. In the end, he traveled about 1,600 miles during this journey.

As a result of Franklin's survey work, stone mile markers were placed along the BOSTON POST ROAD—and other roads as well.

Franklin used an instrument called an **odometer** to measure the distance between postal stations. Franklin's odometer was attached to the back wheel of his horse-drawn carriage. It was a geared device that kept track of how many times the carriage wheel turned. After every 400 revolutions of the wheel, the odometer would record one mile. By the time Postmaster Franklin finished his tour, he had an accurate survey of the roads of his time.

A stone marker along the Boston Post Road

Credit: John Phelan (CC BY 3.0)

The Odometer Through History

People have always been curious about how far their travels take them. Ben Franklin didn't invent the odometer. Odometers have been around since Roman times. An architect and engineer named Vitruvius (c. 80–15 BCE) developed the first one. It had a wheel mounted in a frame. When someone pushed it along the ground, it dropped a pebble into a container each time the wheel revolved once. This allowed someone to measure how far it had traveled. An inventor named Zhang Heng (78–139 CE) came up with China's first odometer during the first or second century CE. This odometer had a figure that would strike a drum every 0.31 miles as it traveled. Some sources say that the odometer Ben Franklin used was one he designed himself. Whether he did or not, by attaching an odometer to his wagon wheel axle, Franklin gained a lot of information about distances—centuries before cars had computerized odometers built in!

Besides figuring out better routes, Franklin came up with another way to improve the speed of mail delivery. He arranged to have postal riders travel at night. Why do you think this made a difference?

Franklin's innovations to the postal system were incredibly successful. He was able to cut down how long it took a letter to get from Philadelphia to New York City to just one day!

Franklin and his fellow postmaster, William Hunter (died 1761), also made the postal service **profitable** for the first time. Using math, Franklin came up with a rate chart that calculated how much postage to charge based on the weight of the item being mailed and the distance it had to travel. Makes sense, right? A lighter letter traveling to the next town should be cheaper to mail than a heavier one traveling a great distance. Before Franklin's time, such rules about postage fees didn't exist.

Look at Franklin's rate chart from 1765.

🔎 postal museum
Franklin rate

PS

WORDS TO KNOW

Second Continental Congress: delegates from the colonies who met to discuss whether America should declare its independence in 1775.

Gulf Stream: a warm ocean current that starts in the Gulf of Mexico and stretches along the eastern coast of the United States before crossing the Atlantic Ocean, where it is called the North Atlantic Current.

current: the steady flow of water in one direction.

In 1774, the British government fired Franklin from his job as postmaster. Not because it was unhappy with his work, but because it thought his writings supported American independence instead of the British crown. At the time, he was earning more than £700 per year—that's the equivalent of more than $112,500 in 2020!

Luckily for Franklin, he wasn't out of a well-paying postal job for long. The following year, he became postmaster general of the independent united colonies. This put him in charge of all the post offices between Massachusetts and Georgia.

In 1789, the United States had **75 POST OFFICES. In 2018,** it had **26,365!**

The **Second Continental Congress** appointed him to this position, though he held it only until 1776, when he headed to France to serve as American ambassador.

INTRODUCING THE GULF STREAM

Ben Franklin put a lot of time and effort into finding more efficient travel routes during his work as postmaster. But his interest in speedier travel went beyond postal roads. In 1768, Franklin was doing work in London as part of his deputy postmaster general job. Once again, his curiosity led to some serious research. His question involved the speed of ships crossing the Atlantic Ocean.

Franklin had a cousin named Timothy Folger who was a merchant ship captain. He asked Folger why ships such as his traveled from Europe to the American colonies so much faster than British mail ships. The answer had to do with something we now call the **Gulf Stream**.

The Gulf Stream is a long, powerful, warm ocean **current**. It begins in the Gulf of Mexico in the south and flows around Florida's tip into the Atlantic Ocean. It then continues to flow north along the eastern coast of the United States toward Newfoundland before crossing the North Atlantic—where it is called the North Atlantic Current—and reaching the west coast of Europe, including England.

The Gulf Stream carries almost 100 TIMES as much water as the combined flow of all Earth's rivers!

A map of the Gulf Stream drawn by Franklin and James Poupard, 1786

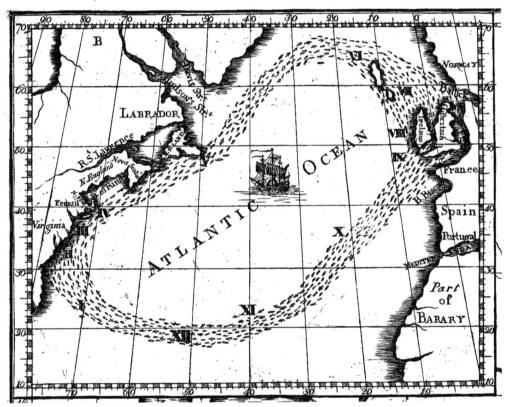

Based on conversations with his cousin, it's clear that Ben Franklin was far from the first person to know about the Gulf Stream.

Take a very high bird's-eye view of ocean currents, including the Gulf Stream. Did Franklin get his map right?

🔎 NASA perpetual ocean

PS

WORDS TO KNOW

gyre: a giant circular ocean current.

dense: describes something that is tightly packed.

In 1513, Spanish explorer Ponce de León (1474–1521) was the first European to write about the Gulf Stream, though it didn't have a name yet. He noted how his ships kept getting caught up in an odd current that seemed even stronger than the wind.

It seems strange that Spain's leaders were not interested in Ponce de León's discovery of this speedy ocean current. Does that mean European explorers never took advantage of the Gulf Stream? No. They gathered knowledge and used the current to help their ships go faster. A ship that stays in the Gulf Stream traveling in a northeastward direction could go almost twice as fast as one not using the current. And yet no one even named it until Ben Franklin came onto the scene. He called it the "Gulph Stream."

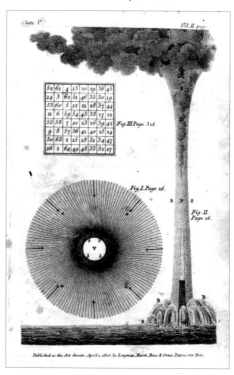

A sketch of water spouts by Ben Franklin, c. 1750

COUSIN COLLABORATION & A COOL CHART

Ben Franklin was keen to pick his cousin's brain about the Gulf Stream. Folger knew a lot about this current from his experiences on a whaling ship. Whalers had discovered that whales often swam along the edges of this current because lots of fish and squid were found there.

In October 1768, Franklin and Folger had extensive conversations about the Gulf Stream. Folger told Franklin that it was great to travel in the current when sailing from America to Europe. This made a ship travel much faster. But on the return journey from Europe to the colonies, the current worked against ships. Sailing in the Gulf Stream slowed a ship down significantly.

Funnily enough, when traveling on a whaling ship himself, Folger had come across mail packet ships heading west toward America. The whaling captains even told the mail ship captains to move out of the current. But, as Folger told Franklin, the packet ship captains believed "they were too wise to be counseled by simple American fishermen." Bad choice!

Earth has five major OCEANIC GYRES.

What Causes the Gulf Stream?

It may seem strange that an ocean current can move water all the way from the Gulf of Mexico to England. The Gulf Stream is caused by a vast system of strong winds and circular currents, known as oceanic **gyres**. Oceans are constantly moving water from one place to another with their currents. The Gulf Stream moves warm water from the Gulf of Mexico as far north as the Norwegian Sea. As the warm water arrives in the north, it causes the colder, more **dense** water to sink and start moving southward. This cold water flows at the bottom of the ocean until it eventually reaches Antarctica.

WORDS TO KNOW

chart: a map or detailed plan.

fathom: a unit of length equaling 6 feet, mainly used to measure water depth.

Ben Franklin thought it would be a good idea to share information about the Gulf Stream. He asked his cousin to sketch the Gulf Stream's path onto an existing **chart**. Folger also wrote directions to help future ships avoid this powerful current when heading from Europe to America.

Franklin wanted mail packet captains to get this information as soon as possible. He arranged to have copies printed in London in 1769. This was the first of three versions of the chart that were printed between 1769 and 1786.

Look at the Franklin-Folger Chart of Gulf Stream of 1769.

🔎 LOC Franklin Folger Gulf Stream

OCEAN SCIENCE

Benjamin Franklin was captivated by the idea of using the Gulf Stream to make sea journeys faster. He was also the first person to do a scientific study of the Gulf Stream.

Franklin had many questions about this ocean current. How big was it? How did the temperatures within the current compare to the surrounding ocean water? He wanted to gain hands-on knowledge of the Gulf Stream. Luckily, he was able to conduct experiments during his voyages across the Atlantic Ocean.

In March 1775, Franklin headed from Europe back to America. His grandson Temple was traveling with him aboard the packet ship *Pennsylvania*. Temple helped with Franklin's Gulf Stream research. They lowered a thermometer down the ship's side into the ocean water while in the Gulf Stream three or four times daily. Then, they recorded the information on a chart. Franklin also measured the temperature of the water when the ship moved out of the Gulf Stream's range. By tracking this data, they could see that the waters of the Gulf Stream were warmer than those surrounding it.

Another way Franklin could detect when the ship had crossed the Gulf Stream was with wine. What? During his trans-Atlantic voyages, wine bottles were stored in ocean water just below the waterline but against the ship's hull. The wine was warmer when the ship was sailing in the Gulf Stream and cooler when it was outside the current!

Benjamin Franklin crossed the Atlantic Ocean EIGHT TIMES. His first ocean crossing was at age 18 and his LAST AT 79.

In 1776, Franklin headed to France. Again, he measured the ocean temperatures. Sometime between 1780 and 1783, he had a second chart of the Gulf Stream printed in Paris.

Benjamin Franklin took his last trip across the Atlantic in 1785. He was 79. On this voyage, he had another question. Did the warm temperatures of the Gulf Stream extend to the deeper ocean depths? He used an empty bottle with a cork at its end to find out. He lowered this bottle down to a depth of 35 **fathoms**. The water pressure forced the cork inside the bottle, which filled with water. Franklin brought the bottle back up and measured the water temperature. It turned out to be 6 degrees Fahrenheit cooler than the surface ocean water. He conducted a similar experiment using a keg that had two valves. This also confirmed that the deeper water was cooler.

A Cavendish thermometer, similar to what Franklin would have used.
Credit: NOAA

Despite the old-fashioned scientific equipment, Franklin's information about the location and temperature of the Gulf Stream was fairly accurate.

In addition to taking notes on water temperature, Franklin recorded his observations of the colors of ocean water. He suggested that navigators would be wise to bring thermometers with them to use as instruments to help guide their voyages. He put together his various ocean research findings into a letter to a French scientific colleague. These were published in 1786 under the title "Maritime Observations." This publication included ideas about the Gulf Stream, of course, as well as about boating technology, food at sea, and more. It also included a third chart of the Gulf Stream.

This chart is different from the earlier ones in a few ways. First, it uses a different map **projection**. Second, the Gulf Stream appears narrower in this version. Third, the engraver added some decorative elements, such as little ships and an image of Franklin himself having a chat with Neptune, god of the sea.

Take a closer look at Franklin's 1786 map of the Gulf Stream. What do you notice about it?

🔎 LOC Franklin 1786 gulf map

PS

Franklin's Return to Philadelphia, 1785
Credit: Jean Leon Gerome Ferris (1863–1930)

Franklin was not 100-percent correct with everything he said about the Gulf Stream. For example, he described the current as "a river in the ocean." This isn't quite right. However, the Gulf Stream does have similarities to a river. Its waters are channeled in a particular direction and pick up speed because of a variety of factors. These factors include the planet's **rotation**, the **prevailing winds**, and colder currents located both around and below the Gulf Stream.

In general, today's scholars think that the 1769 chart does **A BETTER JOB** of representing Timothy Folger's **knowledge of the current and the surrounding environment** than the 1786 one. Why? Because of modifications the engraver made to the **GULF STREAM CHART**.

As Franklin grew older and slowed his travels, he became more attentive to an interest that he'd had since he was young—health. In the next chapter, we'll discover some of the innovative ways he came up with to stay healthy.

ESSENTIAL QUESTION

What do you think Benjamin Franklin would think about traveling in airplanes?

A Foodie Invention

Franklin loved food. He hated waste. And he traveled quite a bit by sea. One of his lesser-known inventions is the divided soup bowl. How might you avoid spilling soup when eating on a ship? His idea was to have mini-bowls (which look like small indentations) around the edge of the main bowl. If the ship took a sudden dip, the soup would not spill over the bowl's edge as it would with a normal bowl. Instead, it would flow into the mini-bowls around the edge of the bowl. Perfect for slurping.

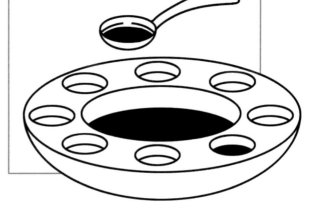

TAKE A RIDE IN AN
OCEAN CURRENT

Ben Franklin observed the Gulf Stream on his voyages between Europe and America. Take your own voyage of discovery making currents at home.

Caution: Have an adult help with the boiling water parts of this experiment.

❯ **Fill your baking dish with cold water until it is about one-third full.** Add a couple of drops of blue food coloring but be careful not to make the water too dark. You want to be able to view the currents as they form.

❯ **Add about 1½ cups of ice to the cold water in the dish.** Stir and let sit for about 3 to 4 minutes so some of the ice has time to melt. You want the water in the dish to be very cold.

❯ **While the ice is melting, boil 3 to 4 cups of water.** Add several of drops of red food coloring to the boiled water, until the color is bright.

❯ **With an adult's help, slowly pour some of the boiling water into one corner of the baking dish.** What happens? How does the hot water affect the movement of the cold water?

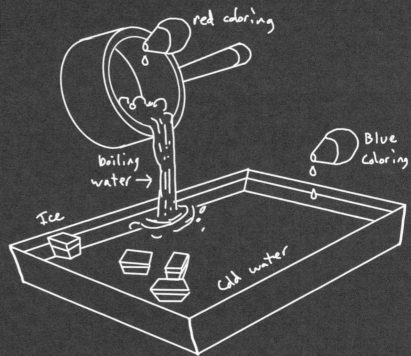

Think Like Ben!

Repeat this experiment, but before adding the ice or boiling water, sprinkle some dried herbs such as basil or oregano into the cold water. What happens?

MAP
YOUR PATH

Ben Franklin surveyed postal routes and mapped the Gulf Stream. Can you create a map showing at least one route between your house and the closest post office?

> **Brainstorm at least one way that you could get from your house to the closest post office, without looking at any maps.** In your science journal, sketch out the route that you would take. Try to name the streets you would take and mark off any landmarks you might pass along the way, such as friends' houses, coffee shops, or parks. Use your markers or colored pencils to make your map more interesting.

The first United States 5-CENT STAMP, issued in 1847, featured **Ben Franklin's image.**

> **Estimate in minutes how long it would take you to travel both on foot and in a car using your route.** How many miles do you think you have to cover to get from your house to the post office?

> **Using Google Maps, type in your home address and the name of your local post office.** Print out a map of the route. On another piece of paper print out the directions for the suggested route. Be sure to include the estimated times for walking and driving, as well as the accurate distance given by the app.

> **How did the different maps compare?** What could you have done differently in your map? Is it possible to take public transportation (bus or train) for any part of the journey between your house and the post office? If so, can you create a new set of directions, including the distances, that includes the segment using public transportation?

Think Like Ben!

Map a different route from your house to the post office. For a bigger challenge, can you make a map of your whole town or a 3-D map made from materials you find around the house?

DESIGN AN
UNBREAKABLE PACKAGE

As postmaster, it was Ben Franklin's job to get mail to its destination quickly. But what about safely? In this activity you'll try to figure out what materials would be best for transporting fragile cargo—eggs—in the post.

❯ **Think about what kinds of packaging are used to deliver fragile items through the mail.** Find some supplies you could use, including recycled materials.

❯ **In your science journal, sketch out some possible designs for a package that would help to prevent an egg from breaking if the package was dropped.**

❯ **Create your package, place an egg inside, and tape the package.**

❯ **Raising your arms as high as you can, drop the package onto the ground.** What happens? Did the packaging protect the egg? If not, what could you do to improve the packaging design?

In 1994, David Donoghue threw an egg from a helicopter **FROM 700 FEET.** This is the world record for longest egg-drop **without breaking!**

Think Like Ben!

Design some packaging that could protect two or three eggs all inside one package. Once you've built the package, drop it again. Did your fragile cargo break?

Egg-Drop Competitions

Around the globe kids and adults participate in egg-drop competitions. Many different designs work well to protect the eggs when dropped from a height. Plastic straws and cardboard are commonly used materials in these competitions. Why do you think that is the case?

Chapter 6

HEALTH

IS IT TRUE THAT AT ONE POINT, YOU TRIED TO BE A VEGETARIAN?

I DID FOR A TIME AND IT BROUGHT ME SOME BENEFIT. BUT I WENT BACK TO MY OLD WAYS AFTER BEING STUCK ON A SHIP WITH NOT MUCH MORE THAN FISH TO EAT.

I CAN SEE HOW THAT WOULD BE TOUGH.

Diet. Disease. Death. Benjamin Franklin was interested in all of these topics during the course of his life, even though he was quite healthy overall. Franklin chose to look at health in a scientific way—through observation, analysis, and experimentation.

In the twenty-first century, much is written on the connection between food and health. **Vegetarian** diets are becoming more and more popular. The world-famous Mayo Clinic states on its website that the health benefits of a vegetarian diet include a reduced risk of diabetes, heart disease, and even some types of cancer. But, more than three centuries ago, Franklin wouldn't have known that. So why did he go through a period of being a vegetarian as a teenager?

ESSENTIAL QUESTION

How did Ben Franklin advance the medical knowledge of his time?

At 16 years old, Ben found a book by Thomas Tyron (1634–1703) that advocated a vegetarian diet. This was very unusual in Colonial America. Ben prepared his own food, including rice, boiled potatoes, and **hasty pudding**.

WORDS TO KNOW

vegetarian: someone who does not eat any meat but does eat eggs or dairy products.

hasty pudding: a mushy dish containing cornmeal or wheat flour mixed with milk or water.

vegan: a vegetarian who won't eat anything that comes from an animal, such as dairy or eggs.

dementia: a group of brain diseases that cause the gradual decline in a person's ability to think and remember.

nutrient: a substance in food and soil that living things need to live and grow.

respiratory: having to do with breathing.

transpiration: the process in which plants give off water vapor through tiny holes in their leaves. Franklin used it to mean an exchange of air.

virus: a non-living, microscopic particle that can cause disease.

Are you a vegetarian? What kinds of meals do you like to eat?

By not eating meat, Ben saved money and used the leftover cash to buy books. He also found he had more time to read and study. Why? Instead of spending time eating big, heavy meals, he chowed down on raisins and biscuits and studied at the same time.

Franklin observed some changes in his own body. He noticed that his mind was clearer and that he was able to learn concepts in math that he hadn't been able to grasp before his vegetarian period.

Is there a scientific connection between brain function and a vegetarian diet? Researchers disagree. But some data shows that people who are lifelong vegetarians or **vegans** are less at risk for **dementia** than meat eaters. Some researchers, however, say that a plant-based diet is not good for brain health because choline, a **nutrient** essential to brain health, is lacking in such a diet. We are still learning the answer to this question!

Was Ben Franklin on to something ahead of his time? Perhaps.

Franklin did not remain a vegetarian for long. While heading to New York in the fall of 1723, he ran into some trouble. The wind died down and his ship was unable to move, stuck off the Rhode Island coast. The crew caught lots of cod, and when it was frying, the smell became too tempting for young Ben. After dining on the tasty fish, he followed a vegetarian diet only occasionally.

THE COMMON COLD

Have you ever had a cold? Even the great Benjamin Franklin got colds. When he was a young man, his most serious health troubles were **respiratory** illnesses. As a result, he became interested in the common cold and what caused it.

While part of **BEN'S MOTIVATION** for being vegetarian was the health benefits, it was also a **FINANCIAL DECISION**. It was cheaper to avoid meat, fish, or fowl.

During the eighteenth century, most people believed that dampness and wet clothing caused colds. Franklin challenged that idea—sailors were always in wet clothes and yet they seemed to stay fairly healthy.

He came up with the following explanation: "People often catch cold from one another when shut up together in close rooms, coaches, etc., and when sitting near and conversing so as to breathe in each other's **transpiration**." Was this idea on the right track? Absolutely! Franklin's theory about what caused the common cold fits in nicely with what we know about **viruses** today—including COVID-19.

Of course, Franklin being Franklin, he came up with ideas on how to avoid getting a cold. Tip number one was fresh air! Even during winter, Franklin believed it essential to have some time with the windows open.

WORDS TO KNOW

smallpox: a contagious disease caused by a virus. Patients have a fever and inflamed blisters that often leave scars.

contagious: easy to catch.

epidemic: a disease that hits large groups at the same time and spreads quickly.

pandemic: an epidemic that happens across a large area, on more than one continent, infecting many people in many countries at the same time.

vaccine: medicine designed to keep a person from getting a particular disease, usually given by needle.

He also was a fan of air baths. "I rise almost every morning and sit in my chamber without any clothes on whatever, half an hour or hour, according to the season, either reading or writing. This practice is not in the least painful, but, on the contrary, agreeable . . . . I shall therefore call it for the future a bracing or tonic bath." Not how most people picture a founding father!

Franklin also suggested exercise and bathing to avoid getting colds, as well as not eating or drinking too much. Long before people looked to the internet for health advice, Benjamin Franklin was giving it out.

SMALLPOX AND SAD TIMES

Have you ever heard of **smallpox**? It's a very **contagious** disease caused by a virus that resulted in serious problems for people for more than 3,000 years. Symptoms include a fever and a distinctive-looking skin rash. Roughly three out of 10 people with smallpox died, and survivors often had permanent scars as a result of the disease. Some were made blind.

During the 1700s, smallpox **epidemics** broke out in Boston and Philadelphia several times. A merchant ship carrying someone infected with smallpox would often arrive in a commercial town. The disease would then sweep through the town.

A recent study in the *American Journal of Medicine* found that women who walked for **30 MINUTES A DAY** for a year had half as many colds as women who didn't exercise.

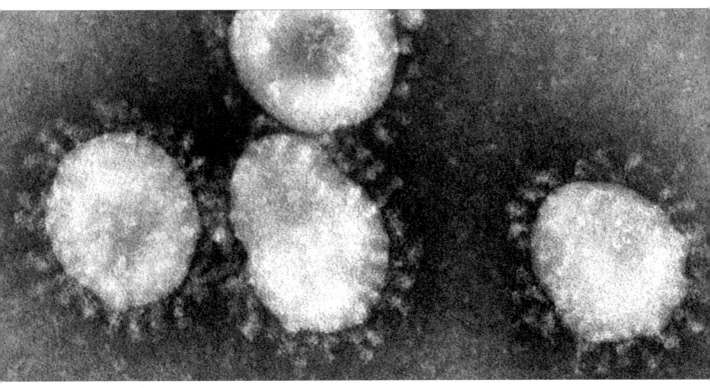

We now know that colds and flus are caused by viruses, including the coronavirus pictured here. In 2020 and 2021, a coronavirus caused a **pandemic** that sickened or killed millions of people around the world.

Smallpox mainly spread when people were in close, face-to-face contact. An infected person—who might not know they were infected at the time—would sneeze or cough. Tiny droplets from their nose or mouth spread to others. Unfortunately, smallpox patients were contagious until the last scabs fell off their blisters. Infected clothing or bedding could also infect other people.

COVID-19

COVID-19 is an illness that started making people sick at the very end of 2019. This virus causes people to have flu-like symptoms and spreads easily between people. Common symptoms are fever, cough, as well as trouble breathing. Researchers worked hard throughout 2020 to develop a **vaccine** to stop this deadly disease.

WORDS TO KNOW

inoculation: vaccination to protect against a disease.

immune system: the system that protects the body against disease and infection.

pathogen: a bacteria, virus, or other microorganism that can cause disease.

antibodies: proteins that help the immune system fight infections or bacteria.

pustule: an inflamed blister full of pus.

In 1721, smallpox broke out in Boston. An African servant named Onesimus (late 1600s–1700s) worked for a Boston clergyman named Cotton Mather (1663–1728). Onesimus told Mather about how smallpox **inoculation** was used in West Africa. Mather got a doctor in Boston to try it out. The people who were inoculated had a much lower death rate than those who hadn't been.

In 1721, James Franklin's newspaper, the *New England Courant*, criticized smallpox inoculation. After all, you could be inoculated and still get smallpox and die. Plus, a huge smallpox outbreak did not happen every year. Some people chose not to be inoculated since it wasn't a risk-free decision.

How Inoculations Work—Now and Then

Have you ever gotten a shot at the doctor's office? Perhaps it was to prevent a disease such as the measles or even the flu. An inoculation trains your **immune system** to both recognize and fight **pathogens**. These pathogens could be viruses, such as the one that causes smallpox, or bacteria. When you get a vaccine, weakened or dead molecules from the pathogen are introduced to your body. This triggers an immune response—the vaccine causes the body to produce **antibodies** to fight the disease.

Inoculation was done very differently in Ben Franklin's time. A string was drawn through a smallpox victim's **pustule** and dried for later use. When someone needed to be inoculated, the doctor would make an incision in their arm and pull the string through that incision. This would infect the person with a weakened form of smallpox so they often ended up getting a milder form of smallpox and had a lower risk of death from the disease. It was not perfect, but it was better than no treatment.

Ben Franklin was a logical thinker who used data to help him make decisions. He wrote about inoculations in the *Pennsylvania Gazette* in 1730 and gave his strong support for inoculations. He also published statistics showing how effective they were. He used numbers to demonstrate that most people who had been inoculated survived and were better for it.

Read a paragraph that Franklin published in the *Pennsylvania Gazette* after his son's death. Why would he want to clear up a rumor about inoculation?

🔍 Founders Franklin death son

PS

Very sadly, Benjamin Franklin had a 4-year-old son named Franky who died of smallpox in 1736. Franklin had planned to inoculate him but Franky had been ill, so they waited. This decision to wait haunted Franklin for the rest of his life.

Some say that Franklin's wife, Deborah, had not wanted to risk inoculating her son. It is also said that Franky's death hurt his parents' marriage.

WORDS TO KNOW

satirical: something designed to make fun of and show a person's weaknesses.

eradicate: to put an end to.

involuntarily: not being done by choice or willingly.

paralysis: the loss of the ability to move or feel a part of the body.

Benjamin Franklin continued to learn about smallpox and inoculations after Franky's death. He wrote letters to doctors and politicians in both Colonial America and Europe to promote inoculation. He also was a coauthor on a manual titled *Some Account of the Success of Inoculation for the Small-Pox in England and America: Together with Plain Instructions.* This manual came out in 1759 and was distributed in America and Europe.

Franklin expressed regret at not inoculating his son. He strongly suggested that other parents inoculate their kids. Years after Franklin's loss, other founding fathers heeded his advice.

A **satirical** painting of people getting the smallpox inoculation

Credit: Wellcome Collection (CC BY 4.0 International)

In 1777, George Washington (1732–1799) ordered his soldiers to be inoculated against smallpox. And in 1782, Thomas Jefferson, who had read a lot on the subject of smallpox, inoculated himself and his own kids.

Improvements continued to be made to the process of smallpox inoculation after Franklin's era. And smallpox was finally **eradicated** in 1979. Ben Franklin would have been delighted to hear that!

"In 1736 I lost one of my sons, **A FINE BOY** of four years old, by the smallpox taken in the common way. I long **REGRETTED BITTERLY** and still regret that I had not given it to him by inoculation."

—Benjamin Franklin in his autobiography

ELECTRICITY AS MEDICINE

When people think of Ben Franklin and electricity, they imagine his kite experiment or lightning rod invention. But did you know that he also used electricity for medical purposes?

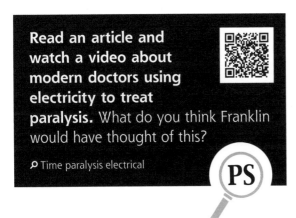

Read an article and watch a video about modern doctors using electricity to treat **paralysis.** What do you think Franklin would have thought of this?

🔎 Time paralysis electrical

From the early 1700s, medical experts knew that an electrical shock could make a person's muscles **involuntarily** twitch and contract. Many folks wished that "electrical fire" could be used to cure **paralysis**. Could a charge through a paralyzed arm or leg restore the limb's movement or regenerate muscle?

Franklin had his doubts, but he was willing to follow the science. He wanted to know if electrical therapies might help patients who came to him seeking help. To experiment, he used his electrostatic generator and a Leyden jar.

WORDS TO KNOW

lame: unable to walk or move normally because of an illness or injury.

kidney stones: hard masses formed in the kidneys, usually made up of calcium compounds.

deposits: a body or layer of accumulated matter.

ureter: the duct through which urine passes from the kidney to the bladder.

anatomy: the science of the structure of living things.

catheter: a flexible tube used for removing fluid, typically inserted through an opening into a body cavity (especially the bladder).

urethra: the tube that carries urine from the bladder out of the body.

temple spectacles: glasses with rigid side pieces to keep them in place.

In December 1757, Franklin wrote a letter to Sir John Pringle (1707–1782), a member of the Royal Society and later a royal physician. He described the treatments he'd administered.

"My method was, to place the patient first in a chair on an electric stool, and draw a number of large strong sparks from all parts of the affected limb or side. Then I fully charg'd two 6 gallon jars, each of which had about 3 square feet of surface coated and I sent the united shock of these thro' the affected limb or limbs, repeating the stroke commonly three times each day."

Franklin observed that, at first, there seemed to be more warmth in the **lame** limbs after the treatment. The limbs also seemed stronger and better able to move voluntarily—but only for a short time. He concluded that electrical therapy had no long-term or permanent advantages for paralysis patients.

"There was hardly a field of **HUMAN ENDEAVOR** that the 18th-century American printer, author, diplomat and scientist, Benjamin Franklin, worked in without some benefit to those **WHO CAME AFTER HIM**."
—Edward Huth, writer

MEDICAL INVENTIONS

It probably comes as no surprise that Benjamin Franklin came up with medical inventions. One such invention had to do with his older brother John, who suffered from **kidney stones**. These are hard **deposits** made up of salts and minerals that can form inside a person's kidneys. They can affect different parts of the urinary tract from the bladder to the kidneys to the **ureter** (the tube that connects these parts). It can be very painful for someone to pass kidney stones.

Skeletons in Ben Franklin's Basement

Benjamin Franklin lived at 36 Craven Street in London for almost 16 years, between 1757 and 1775. More than two centuries later, people doing repairs on the home came across more than 1,200 pieces of bone in the basement. These remains came from more than 15 different people. It turns out that a friend of Franklin's named William Hewson (1739–1774) ran an **anatomy** school there. It's unlikely Franklin was involved with the school, but some historians speculate that he probably peeked in at some point. After all, he was super curious!

People being treated for bladder problems such as kidney stones might have to use a thin tube called a **catheter** to have urine drained from their bladder. The tube is inserted into a patient's **urethra**. Back in Franklin's time, catheters were made of metal and were rigid. Poor John Franklin had to use one of these tubes daily. Ouch!

In 1752, Ben invented a flexible catheter. He enlisted the help of a local silversmith to make this new device. It consisted of different segments of tubes connected together in such a way that they could bend. It was much less painful for the patient.

NEW KIND OF GLASSES

Like many people, as Franklin got older, his vision got worse. People said that he wore **temple spectacles** some of the time when he was living in London in the late 1750s. After 1776, Franklin wore glasses all the time. But he needed two sets. He got frustrated with having to switch between the glasses that let him see things in the distance and those that let him see things close up. What did he do? Invent a new kind of glasses, of course.

WORDS TO KNOW

bifocals: glasses with lenses that are divided into two parts. The upper half is for looking at things far away and the lower half is for reading or for looking at things that are near.

optician: a person who makes and supplies eyeglasses and contact lenses to correct someone's vision.

epitaph: an inscription on a gravestone that describes the person buried there.

Franklin invented **bifocals**, known as "double spectacles," in 1784.

As with many of his inventions, Franklin got a local craftsman to help him—in this case, a glasscutter. He took the lenses from both pairs of glasses and cut them in half, then placed half of each lens into a single frame. The bottom lens was for close-up objects and for reading, and the top was for distance.

In 1784, Franklin acknowledged that without his glasses, he couldn't "distinguish a letter even of large print."

Franklin was quite pleased with his bifocals. But not just because they made reading easier. He told a friend that he found his new glasses to be especially useful when having dinner in France.

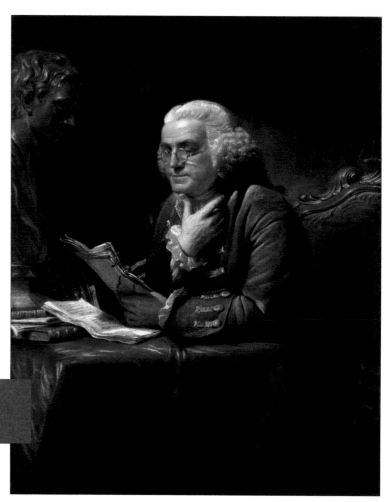

Benjamin Franklin wearing glasses, 1767
Credit: David Martin (1737–1797)

Why? They allowed him not only to see his food but also to check out peoples' facial expressions when eating. Being able to see facial expressions allowed Franklin to figure out what words were being said. "I understand French better by the help of my Spectacles."

Some historians do not believe that Benjamin Franklin was the one who invented bifocals. They think bifocals were already available from London **opticians** in the 1760s.

From common colds to inoculation to bifocals, Benjamin Franklin did much to advance medical knowledge. His research and inventions certainly made life more comfortable and healthier for people from his time to the present. The Medical Society of London even honored Franklin in 1785 for his contributions to the field.

When he was **22 YEARS OLD**, Franklin wrote his own **epitaph.** "The Body of B. Franklin Printer; Like the Cover of an old Book, **Its Contents torn out, And stript of its Lettering and Gilding, Lies here, Food for** Worms. But the Work shall not be wholly lost: For it will, as he believ'd, appear once more, In a new & more perfect Edition, Corrected and Amended By the Author." His **ACTUAL EPITAPH IS MUCH SHORTER**: "Benjamin and Deborah Franklin."

From boyhood to old age, Benjamin Franklin was a true scientist. He asked questions, sought out answers, and worked to improve the lives of all people through his experimentation and inventions. He was not afraid to fail and allowed himself to try new things, even if his ideas didn't always work out as he had planned.

Through his work as a printer, postmaster, diplomat, scientist, and inventor, he became what many would call the most influential American of his era. For most of us, not a day goes by in which we are not affected by something that Benjamin Franklin studied or created.

ESSENTIAL QUESTION

How did Ben Franklin advance the medical knowledge of his time?

GET YOUR
HEART GOING

Ben Franklin was a big believer in the importance of exercise. He exercised in a variety of ways, such as weightlifting and swimming. In this activity, you can compare different types of exercise to see which ones boost your heart rate the most.

❯ **Begin by making a list of some types of exercise you can easily do at home.**

❯ **To find your resting heart rate, you'll need to check your pulse with a partner.** Place your index and middle fingers on your neck, just to the side of your windpipe. Once you find your pulse, count the number of beats you feel in 15 seconds. Have your partner tell you when the 15 seconds begin and end. Multiply that number times four to calculate the number of beats per minute. Write down your resting rate in your science journal.

❯ **Start with one of your exercises, such as lifting a light weight.** Do this exercise for one minute. Have your partner tell you when to start and stop. When the minute is up, record your heart rate for 15 seconds. Again, multiply this number times four and record your activity and your heart rate in your science journal.

❯ **Repeat step 3 with each of the following: jumping jacks, bouncing a ball, and walking up and down stairs.** Record your findings. Which exercise boosted your heart rate the most? Why do you think that was the case?

❯ **Come up with some other exercise ideas and try a couple of them for 60 seconds, recording your heart rate as in step 3.** Also try non-exercise activities, such as watching TV or playing video games and see how doing them for 60 seconds compares to your resting heart rate.

Think Like Ben!

Have other members of your family or some friends record their resting and post-exercise heart rates. How were their results different from yours? Why do you think this was so? Which exercises do you think are most heart-healthy?

EYE TESTS
FOR ALL

CACHE KIT
° computer with printer
° tape or Blu-Tack
° measuring tape
° at least 2 people to help
° pen and paper

Ben Franklin is famous for inventing bifocals. In this activity, try your hand at being an eye doctor. Find out how good your vision is—and that of some friends and family, too!

Reminder: This activity is not meant to be a substitute for a proper eye exam. You should see a doctor for that.

❯ **Go to the Vision Source website.** Download and print the free eye chart.

❯ **At eye level, tape or tack the eye chart onto a wall that doesn't have windows.** Be sure to get permission before taping anything to the wall.

❯ **Measure 10 feet from the wall.** Have your first "patient" stand there.

🔎 vision source eye chart

❯ **Ask this first patient to cover up one eye.** They can keep their glasses on if they use them for distance vision.

❯ **Ask another person to work as the doctor and point to each line.** The patient should read off the letters aloud. The doctor should keep track of how many letters the patient gets right or wrong. Repeat this going down a line each time. Stop when the patient can't read the letters anymore.

❯ **Write the number of the smallest line where the patient could identify most of the letters correctly.** For example, if the patient could read five out of the eight letters found on line 8, their result would be 20/20. If a person has 20/20 vision, that means he or she can see clearly from a distance of 20 feet.

❯ **Repeat steps 4 through 7 with the patient's other eye and then with both eyes.** How different are the results?

Think Like Ben!

What happens when you have your "patients" try the vision test again from farther away—perhaps 15 feet? You could also repeat the eye testing outside by taping your eye chart to an outdoor wall or tree. How does peoples' visual clarity change at 30 or 40 feet away?

GO OUTSIDE AND
THINK BETTER?

Ben Franklin was a huge advocate for getting fresh air. He also was a big reader. Research shows that spending time outdoors can improve peoples' health—but what about memory? This activity requires you to have a number of participants handy.

❯ **Divide the participants into two groups—indoor and outdoor.**

❯ **Put two people in charge of setting up the small objects and also using the timer.** Assemble one flat surface with 15 objects indoors. Cover these with a tablecloth so no one sees them. Assemble one flat surface with 15 objects outdoors and cover them, too.

❯ **Gather the participants together around the flat surfaces.** Half of them should be in the indoor group and half in the outdoor group. Remove the tablecloth to show the objects. Allow the participants to look at the objects for just 60 seconds. They should not have paper or pens during this time.

❯ **When the 60 seconds have passed, cover the objects up again with the tablecloth.** Ask the participants to write down as many objects as they can remember in two minutes.

❯ **Ask each participant to read quietly for 20 minutes.** During this time, the people in charge of the objects will switch their 15 items—bringing the ones that were outdoors inside and vice versa. Like before, the items will be covered by a tablecloth.

❯ **At the end of the reading period, repeat steps 3 and 4 with the new objects.** Compare the scores for each participant.

❯ **Scientific research shows that exercise boost the memory and thinking skills of people.** Did your experiment support this theory? Did the indoor or outdoor group remember the objects better?

Think Like Ben!

Instead of reading a book for 20 minutes, ask the participants to exercise during the 20 minutes between memory tests. Do the results change?

absorb: to soak up a liquid or take in energy, heat, light, or sound.

advocate: to publicly support.

Age of Enlightenment: the time period when European scientists and philosophers started to examine the world using reason rather than religion.

agent: a person who does business or acts on behalf of others.

almanac: a reference book containing information such as weather forecasts, lists and tables, moon phases and tide charts, short articles, and household tips.

ambassador: someone who represents his or her country.

amber: hard, fossilized resin. Resin is a sticky substance that oozes from trees.

analysis: a careful study.

anatomy: the science of the structure of living things.

antibodies: proteins that help the immune system fight infections or bacteria.

apprentice: a person who works with a master to learn a skill or trade.

arthritis: a medical condition that causes swollen joints, stiffness, and pain.

atmosphere: the blanket of air surrounding the earth.

atom: a very small piece of matter.

attract: a force that draws things closer.

aurora borealis: a natural display of shimmering colors in the night sky, usually only seen in the far north. Also called the northern lights.

ballad: poetic verses set to song.

BCE: put after a date, BCE stands for Before Common Era and counts years down to zero. CE stands for Common Era and counts years up from zero. This book was published in 2021 CE.

bifocals: glasses with lenses that are divided into two parts. The upper half is for looking at things far away and the lower half is for reading or for looking at things that are near.

blueprint: a model or template to follow.

blunt: having a rounded or flat end.

botany: the study of plants.

British Commonwealth: countries associated with Great Britain.

buoy: to keep afloat.

butter churn: a device that spins and converts cream into butter.

catheter: a flexible tube used for removing fluid, typically inserted through an opening into a body cavity (especially the bladder).

centralized: brought under a single authority or control.

chart: a map or detailed plan.

clergyman: a male religious leader, such as a minister or priest, particularly a Christian one.

colony: an area that is controlled by or belongs to another country.

commissioner: an official in charge of a government department.

common law marriage: a marriage through living together for the long term rather than by a civil or religious ceremony.

concentric: having a common center.

conduct: to transfer something such as electricity or heat.

conservation of charge: the scientific concept that electricity has equal amounts of positive and negative charges.

contagious: easy to catch.

Continental Congress: the group of delegates from the American colonies who met during and after the American Revolution. They issued the Declaration of Independence and Articles of Confederation.

contract: to shrink and take up less space.

control: something used as a standard for comparison to check the results of an experiment.

convection: the transfer of heat from one region to another by the movement of a gas or liquid.

crevice: a narrow opening, especially in a rock or wall or where two sides meet.

current: the steady flow of water in one direction.

damper: a plate or valve that regulates the draft in a fireplace or stove.

dementia: a group of brain diseases that cause the gradual decline in a person's ability to think and remember.

dense: describes something that is tightly packed.

deposits: a body or layer of accumulated matter.

deputy: the assistant who normally takes command when their superior is absent.

diplomat: a person who represents one country to another.

duet: a musical composition written for two performers to play.

electrical charge: a force of electricity that can be either positive or negative.

electrical current: the flow of electrons through a material.

electricity: energy created by the movement of electrons between atoms. An atom is a tiny particle of matter. Electrons are particles in an atom that have a negative charge and move around.

electrocute: to injure or kill something by electric shock.

electron: a particle in an atom with a negative charge that moves around the nucleus.

electrostatic machine: a machine used to generate sparks of electricity.

embalm: to preserve a body.

embellishment: a decorative detail or feature added to make something more attractive.

energy-efficient: using less energy to provide the same results.

engineering: using science, math, and creativity to design and build things.

engraving: a type of printing where the design is drawn or etched into the plate instead of the design being raised on the plate.

epidemic: a disease that hits large groups at the same time and spreads quickly.

epitaph: an inscription on a gravestone that describes the person buried there.

eradicate: to put an end to.

expand: to spread out and take up more space.

fathom: a unit of length equaling 6 feet, mainly used to measure water depth.

fluid: a substance such as a gas or a liquid that flows freely and has no fixed shape.

force: a push or a pull that causes a change of motion in an object.

ford: a shallow place in a stream or river that allows people to drive or walk across.

friction: a force that slows down objects when they rub against each other.

Gulf Stream: a warm ocean current that starts in the Gulf of Mexico and stretches along the eastern coast of the United States before crossing the Atlantic Ocean, where it is called the North Atlantic Current.

gyre: a giant circular ocean current.

hasty pudding: a mushy dish containing cornmeal or wheat flour mixed with milk or water.

hemp: the fiber that comes from a tall Asian herb.

immune system: the system that protects the body against disease and infection.

impromptu: unplanned.

induct: to formally admit into an organization.

innovator: a person who introduces new products, ideas, or methods.

inoculation: vaccination to protect against a disease.

inquiry: a search for knowledge or truth.

insulator: a material that prevents heat, sound, or electricity from passing through it easily.

involuntarily: not being done by choice or willingly.

kidney stones: hard masses formed in the kidneys, usually made up of calcium compounds.

lame: unable to walk or move normally because of an illness or injury.

Leyden jar: a storage container for electricity made of glass, foil, and wire.

lightning rod: a metal rod attached to the highest point of a building that attracts lightning and guides it to the ground.

long arm: a mechanical arm invented by Ben Franklin that was used to reach books on high shelves.

lunar eclipse: when the moon, earth, and sun are all lined up in a row so that the earth casts a shadow on the moon.

magnetic field: an invisible area (or field) created by a magnet.

manufacture: to make into a product.

median: the middle value in a list of numbers.

merchant: a person or company involved in the trade of goods, especially one that deals with foreign countries.

molecule: a group of atoms bound together to form matter.

momentum: a force that keeps an object moving after it has begun to move.

moonshine: a type of alcoholic liquor, often made illegally.

moral: concerned with principles of wrong or right behavior.

musicologist: a person who studies music.

natural philosopher: the term once used to describe people interested in science.

neutron: a particle in the nucleus of an atom that has no charge.

nucleus: the center of an atom, made up of protons and neutrons. The plural is nuclei.

nutrient: a substance in food and soil that living things need to live and grow.

odometer: a device that measures the distance traveled, especially by a vehicle.

optician: a person who makes and supplies eyeglasses and contact lenses to correct someone's vision.

palette: a thin, normally oval board with a thumb hole at one end, used by artists to lay and mix paints.

palmetto: a fan palm, particularly one of several that grows from the southern United States to northern South America.

pamphlet: an informative brochure or book.

pandemic: an epidemic that happens across a large area, on more than one continent, infecting many people in many countries at the same time.

paralysis: the loss of the ability to move or feel a part of the body.

particle: a tiny piece of matter.

patent: a document given to the inventor of something that protects them from someone copying their invention.

pathogen: a bacteria, virus, or other microorganism that can cause disease.

phenomena: events, facts, or features of scientific interest that can be observed.

physicist: a scientist who studies physical forces, including matter, energy, and motion, and how these forces interact with each other.

pitch: the lowness or highness of a sound.

polar regions: the areas of the earth around the North and South Poles, within the Arctic and Antarctic Circles.

postmaster general: an official in charge of the post office.

prestigious: inspiring respect and admiration.

prevailing winds: winds from the direction that is predominant during a particular season or at a particular place.

procedure: a series of actions performed in a specific order.

profitable: making money from a business or activity.

projection: a method for representing Earth on a flat surface.

promotional: relating to the publicizing of a product or venture to increase sales or boost public awareness.

propel: to push forward.

property: a characteristic quality or distinctive feature of something.

proton: a particle in the nucleus of an atom that has a positive charge.

prototype: a working model or mock-up that allows engineers to test their solution.

pseudonym: a pen name, or fictitious name used by an author.

pulley: a simple machine consisting of a wheel with a grooved rim that a rope or chain is pulled through to help lift a load.

pustule: an inflamed blister full of pus.

radiate: to spread outward.

reflect: to redirect something that hits a surface, such as heat, light, or sound.

Renaissance man: a person who has many areas of knowledge or talents.

repel: a force that pushes things away.

resistance: a slowing force on something that is moving.

resonant: continuing to produce sound.

respiratory: having to do with breathing.

rotation: a turn all the way around.

satirical: something designed to make fun of and show a person's weaknesses.

Second Continental Congress: delegates from the colonies who met to discuss whether America should declare its independence in 1775.

single-fluid theory of electricity: the theory that electricity flows both within and between objects and that an excess of fluid makes some objects positive, while a lack of fluid makes others negative.

skeptical: doubting the truth or value of an idea or belief.

smallpox: a contagious disease caused by a virus. Patients have a fever and inflamed blisters that often leave scars.

statesman: an experienced political leader.

static electricity: a buildup of an electrical charge on an object, usually produced by friction.

surface area: the total area that the surface of an object occupies.

survey: to examine and record the features of an area of land in order to construct a map or a plan.

swatch: a small sample piece of fabric.

tavern: a place where people can buy food and drink and enjoy each other's company.

technical: relating to scientific or mechanical methods.

temple spectacles: glasses that had rigid side pieces to keep them in place.

theory: a set of ideas to explain something that has happened.

tide: the daily rise and fall of the ocean's water level near a shore.

transpiration: the process in which plants give off water vapor through tiny holes in their leaves. Franklin used it to mean an exchange of air.

trills: rapid alternations between one tone and another, often performed on a long note of a song.

ureter: the duct through which urine passes from the kidney to the bladder.

urethra: the tube that carries urine from the bladder out of the body.

vaccine: medicine designed to keep a person from getting a particular disease, usually given by needle.

vegan: a vegetarian who won't eat anything that comes from an animal, such as dairy or eggs.

vegetarian: someone who does not eat any meat but does eat eggs or dairy products.

virus: a non-living microscopic particle that can cause disease.

work: the amount of energy needed to move an object a certain distance.

Metric Conversions

Use this chart to find the metric equivalents to the English measurements in this book. If you need to know a half measurement, divide by two. If you need to know twice the measurement, multiply by two. How do you find a quarter measurement? How do you find three times the measurement?

English	Metric
1 inch	2.5 centimeters
1 foot	30.5 centimeters
1 yard	0.9 meter
1 mile	1.6 kilometers
1 pound	0.5 kilogram
1 teaspoon	5 milliliters
1 tablespoon	15 milliliters
1 cup	237 milliliters

BOOKS

Byrd, Robert. *Electric Ben: The Amazing Life and Times of Benjamin Franklin*. Dial Books for Young Readers, 2012.

Fleming, Candace. *Ben Franklin's Almanac: Being a True Account of the Good Gentleman's Life*. Anne Schwartz Books Atheneum, 2003.

Fleming, Thomas. *Ben Franklin: Inventing America*. Young Voyageur, 2016.

Gunderson, Jessica. *The Real Benjamin Franklin: The Truth Behind the Legend*. Compass Point Books, 2019.

Higgins, Maria Mihalik. *Benjamin Franklin: Revolutionary Inventor*. Sterling Publishing Company, 2007.

Hirschfeld, Tom, and Leila Hirschfeld. *It's Up to You, Ben Franklin: How I Made the Biggest Decisions of My Life*. Crown Books for Young Readers, 2019.

Krull, Kathleen. *Benjamin Franklin*. Viking, 2013.

Miller, Brandon Marie. *Benjamin Franklin: American Genius: His Life and Ideas with 21 Activities*. Chicago Review Press, 2009.

Osborne, Mary Pope, and Natalie Pope Boyce. *Benjamin Franklin: A Nonfiction Companion to Magic Tree House #32: To the Future, Ben Franklin!* Random House Books for Young Readers, 2019.

MUSEUMS

Benjamin Franklin House in London, England
benjaminfranklinhouse.org

Benjamin Franklin Museum in Philadelphia, PA
nps.gov/inde/planyourvisit/benjaminfranklinmuseum.htm

The Franklin Institute in Philadelphia, PA
www.fi.edu/plan-your-visit

Museum of the American Revolution in Philadelphia, PA
amrevmuseum.org

MUSEUMS (CONTINUED)

National Liberty Museum in Philadelphia, PA
libertymuseum.org/visit/hours-admission

Smithsonian National Museum of American History in Washington, DC
americanhistory.si.edu

Smithsonian National Postal Museum in Washington, DC
postalmuseum.si.edu/exhibits/current/binding-the-nation/
starting-the-system/benjamin-franklin.html

WEBSITES

"Benjamin Franklin." PBS Benjamin Franklin.
pbs.org/benfranklin

"Benjamin Franklin." Time for Kids.
timeforkids.com/g34/benjamin-franklin

"Benjamin Franklin and Electricity."
America's Story—Library of Congress.
americaslibrary.gov/aa/franklinb/aa_franklinb_electric_2.html

"Benjamin Franklin FAQ." Franklin Institute.
fi.edu/benjamin-franklin-faq

"Benjamin Franklin...In his Own Words." Library of Congress.
loc.gov/exhibits/franklin/franklin-scientist.html

"Benjamin Franklin: Writer, Inventor, and Founding Father."
PBS Learning Media.
pbslearningmedia.org/resource/
3ba2723a-f2a0-4ef2-a559-795742ac3118/benjamin-franklin

"Finding Franklin: A Resource Guide." Library of Congress.
loc.gov/rr/program/bib/franklin/loc.html

"Franklin & The House." Benjamin Franklin House.
benjaminfranklinhouse.org/the-house-benjamin-franklin

RESOURCES

SELECTED BIBLIOGRAPHY

"Benjamin Franklin's Inventions." The Franklin Institute.
fi.edu/benjamin-franklin/inventions

Chaplin, Joyce. *The First Scientific American: Benjamin Franklin and the Pursuit of Genius.* Basic Books, 2006.

Eighmey, Rae Katherine. *Stirring the Pot With Benjamin Franklin: A Founding Father's Culinary Adventures.* Smithsonian Books, 2018.

Eschner, Kat. "Benjamin Franklin Was the First to Chart the Gulf Stream." *Smithsonian*, 2017.
smithsonianmag.com/smart-news/benjamin-franklin-was-first-chart-gulf-stream-180963066/

Gensel, Lisa. "The Medical World of Benjamin Franklin."
Journal of the Royal Society of Medicine. 2005: Dec; 98(12) 534-538.
National Center for Biotechnology Information,
ncbi.nlm.nih.gov/pmc/articles/PMC1299336

Goodwin, George. *Benjamin Franklin in London: The British Life Of America's Founding Father.* Yale University Press, 2016.

Heiligman, Deborah. *The Mysterious Ocean Highway: Benjamin Franklin and the Gulf Stream.* Raintree Steck-Vaughn Publishers, 2000.

Hintz, Eric S. "Benjamin Franklin's Inventions."
Smithsonian National Museum of American History,
invention.si.edu/benjamin-franklin-s-inventions

Isaacson, Walter. *Benjamin Franklin: An American Life.* Simon & Schuster, 2004.

Roth, Ginny A. "The First Postmaster General." U.S. National Library of Medicine, 2013.
circulatingnow.nlm.nih.gov/2013/07/26/the-first-postmaster-general-and-inventor-of-a-flexible-urinary-catheter

"The First U.S. Postage Stamp Honoring Benjamin Franklin, Patriot and Postmaster." Smithsonian National Postal Museum,
postalmuseum.si.edu/collections/object-spotlight/franklin.html

Weld, Horatio Hastings, and Benjamin Franklin. *Benjamin Franklin: His Autobiography: With a Narrative of His Public Life and Services.* Harper & Brothers, Publishers, 1848.

ESSENTIAL QUESTIONS

Introduction: What is Benjamin Franklin famous for?

Chapter 1: If an invention doesn't work as planned, is it a failure or a success? Why?

Chapter 2: How are heat and light related to each other?

Chapter 3: How did Ben Franklin change peoples' understanding of electricity?

Chapter 4: How was Franklin an example of the quote, "Necessity is the mother of invention?"

Chapter 5: What do you think Benjamin Franklin would think about traveling in airplanes?

Chapter 6: How did Ben Franklin advance the medical knowledge of his time?

QR CODE GLOSSARY

Page 3: masshist.org/online/silence_dogood/img-viewer.php?item_id=655&img_step=1&tpc=&pid=&mode=large&tpc=&pid=#page1

Page 16: swimmingworldmagazine.com/news/benjamin-franklin-honored-by-international-swimming-hall-of-fame

Page 19: youtube.com/watch?v=PRMeiRIWRnM

Page 21: invention.si.edu/benjamin-franklin-s-inventions

Page 25: fi.edu/benjamin-franklin/the-many-musical-talents-of-benjamin-franklin

Page 33: digitalcollections.powerlibrary.org/cdm/ref/collection/SLP2005001/id/1058

Page 37: youtube.com/watch?v=fVsONlc3OUY

Page 38: exploratorium.edu/learning_studio/auroras/happen.html

QR CODE GLOSSARY (CONTINUED)

Page 44: bbc.co.uk/programmes/p00ksnyn

Page 51: benfranklin300.org/frankliniana/result.php?id=72&sec=0

Page 52: archive.org/details/experimentsobser00fran/page/n8

Page 53: masshist.org/objects/cabinet/december2002/december2002.htm

Page 67: youtube.com/watch?v=RKx1Cx5fog4

Page 69: wikihow.com/Build-a-Pulley

Page 81: postalmuseum.si.edu/object/npm_1984.0493.1

Page 83: nasa.gov/topics/earth/features/perpetual-ocean.html

Page 86: loc.gov/resource/g9112g.ct000753/?r=-0.131,0.096,1.287,0.688,0

Page 88: loc.gov/resource/g9112g.ct000136/?r=-0.075,0.005,1.003,0.575,0

Page 99: founders.archives.gov/documents/Franklin/01-02-02-0025

Page 101: time.com/54146/paralysis-electrical-pulses

Page 107: visionsource.com/patients/free-eye-chart-download

INDEX